AF074331

PORSCHE

VORWORT

Kalifornien – so viele Assoziationen. So viele Worte und Bilder. Jeder kann etwas dazu sagen. Jeder weiß etwas. Das kann erdrücken. Auch bei der Überlegung, was eine CURVES-Ausgabe, geboren auf den Passstraßen der Alpen, zu dieser Region so alles abbilden muss. Nach ein paar Meilen hinter dem Steuer folgt alles einem übernatürlichen Drehbuch. Flow-Power. California Cruisin'. Die Gerade wie eine meditative Fastenkur vor der nächsten Kurve, wie ein Fernrohr auf das Objekt der Begierde gerichtet. Und ist sie dann da, verschlingst Du sie. Verschlingt sie Dich. Es gibt so viel zu entdecken und Du willst alles sehen. Tradition: Zukunft. Dein Kalifornien. Dein Vehikel. Du. *Soulful Driving. Los geht's.*

—

California – so many associations; so many words and images. Everyone has something to say about it. Everyone knows something. It can be overwhelming. Also when considering everything that an edition of CURVES, born on Alpine passes, has to capture of all this. After a few miles at the wheel, it all slots into a mystical screenplay. This is flow power; California cruisin'; the straights taking the form of a meditative fast before the next bend, like a telescope focused on the object of your desire. And then there it is – you devour it. It devours you. There is so much to discover and you want to see it all – tradition, future, ever ahead. Your California. Your vehicle. You. *Soulful driving. Let's go.*

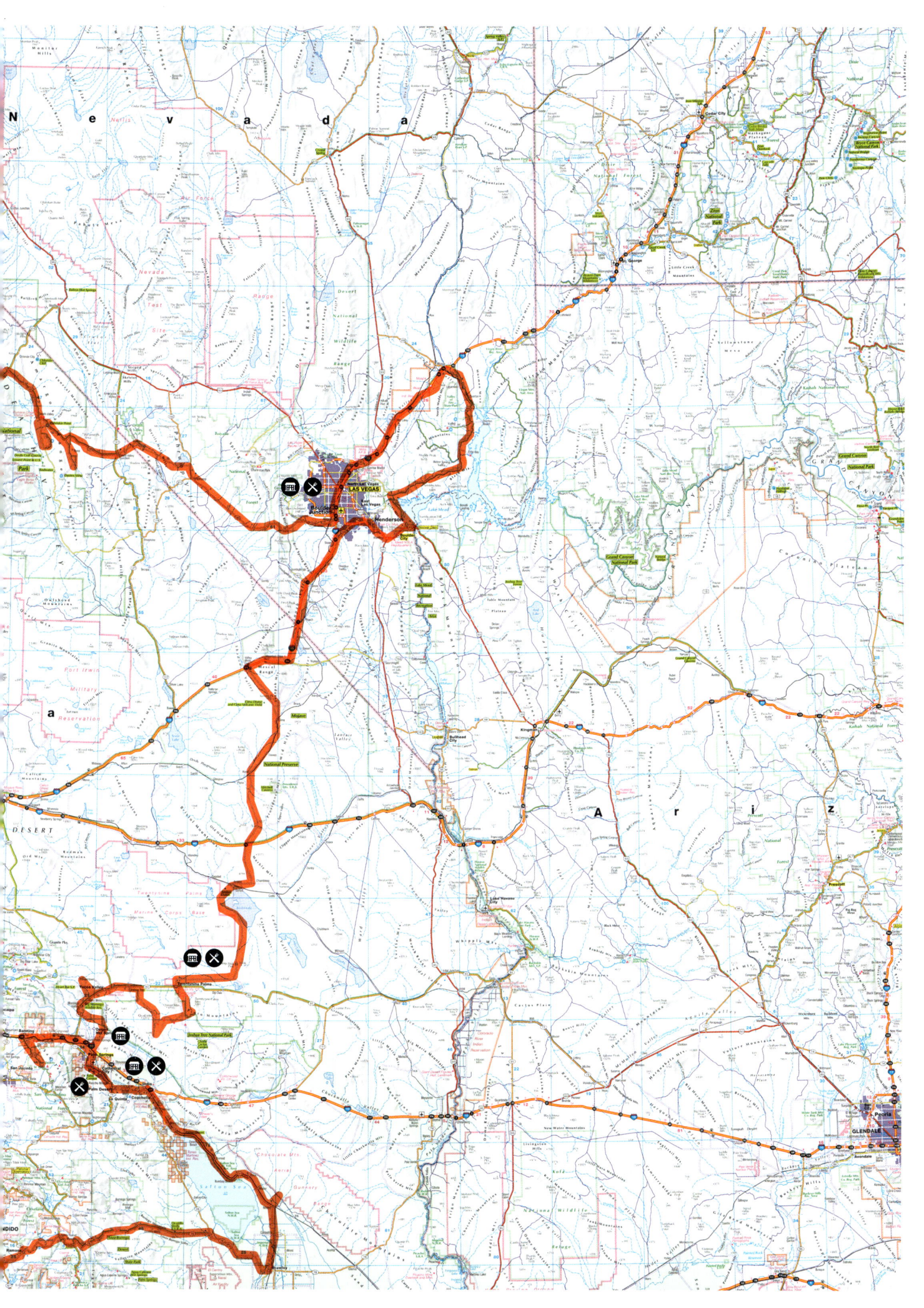

ETAPPE STAGE 1

LOS ANGELES **50**
SAN FRANCISCO **92**

Die Autostadt Los Angeles will ausgiebig erkundet werden. Zwischen Manhattan Beach und Pasadena, Long Beach und Beverly Hills ist ein Auto ideales Fortbewegungsmittel, um der energiegeladenen Metropolregion ganz nahe zu kommen. Am Ende verlassen wir das Stadtgebiet über die Hollywood Hills und den Mulholland Drive nach Norden, landen dann aber bei Malibu wieder an der Pazifikküste. Der PCH, Pacific Coast Highway, ist nun für die nächsten Stunden unsere Sehnsuchtsstraße, zwischen Bergen und Meer fahren wir nach Norden. Dabei sind nicht nur die Fischer- und Surfer-Städte am Meer, die immer noch den legendär coolen California-Lifestyle ausstrahlen eine Reise wert, sondern auch die Straße an sich: Spektakuläre Natur, grandiose Streckenführung – der Highway Number 1 gehört zweifelsfrei zu den schönsten Straßen der Welt. Nach einer intensiven Begegnung mit den belebten und spannenden Städten rund um die Monterey Bay ziehen wir weiter über die Half Moon Bay nach Norden und erreichen mit San Francisco das erste Etappenziel.

The auto city of Los Angeles is crying out to be explored. From Manhattan Beach to Pasadena, Long Beach to Beverly Hills, a car is the ideal means of transportation for getting up close and personal with this energy-charged metropolis. At the end, we leave the city via the Hollywood Hills and Mulholland Drive heading north, landing back at the Pacific coast near Malibu. The PCH, Pacific Coast Highway, is now the road of our desire, taking us northward between mountain and ocean. It's not just the fishing and surfing towns along the coast that make this journey worthwhile, still radiating that legendary, cool Californian lifestyle, but the road in and of itself. Spectacular nature, amazing twists and turns – Highway No. 1 is without doubt one of the most beautiful roads in the world. Following an intense encounter with the vibrant and exciting towns around Monterey Bay, we continue north via Half Moon Bay, reaching the end of our first stage in San Francisco.

ETAPPE STAGE 2

SAN FRANCISCO **98**
YOSEMITE **108**

San Francisco gehört zu den wohl schönsten und spannendsten Städten der Welt. Auch hier hat eine Stadtrundfahrt mit dem Auto ganz besonderen Reiz – Steve McQueen-Fans dürfte die Berg- und Talfahrt über San Franciscos steile Hügelstraßen natürlich ganz besonders anziehen. Danach verlassen wir die Pazifikküste in Richtung Osten, die Reise geht nun ins historische Kalifornien des Goldrauschs. Vom milden Klima der Küste über die fruchtbaren Ebenen im Hinterland bis ins trockene Land am Fuß der Sierra Nevada durchqueren wir auf dieser Fahrt eine Vielzahl von Klima- und Vegetationszonen, am Ende der Fahrt steht der Aufstieg ins Yosemite Valley. Dieser hochgelegene Nationalpark zieht jedes Jahr über drei Millionen Besucher an; beim Blick in das wilde Tal, umgeben von schroffen Bergriesen, ist schnell klar, weshalb Yosemite zu den Landschafts-Ikonen der gesamten USA gehört.

San Francisco is one of the world's most captivating and thrilling cities. Here, too, a city tour by car has a very particular appeal – Steve McQueen fans are, of course, especially drawn to the ups and downs of San Francisco's steep hill streets. We then leave the Pacific Coast heading eastward. Our journey is now taking us into the historical California of the Gold Rush era. From the mild coastal climate, through the fertile hinterland to the arid prairieland at the foot of the Sierra Nevada, this drive takes us through a wide spectrum of climate and vegetation zones, with the trip culminating in the ascent into Yosemite Valley. This high-altitude national park draws more than three million visitors every year. Just one glance into the wild valley surrounded by rugged mountains is all it takes to see exactly why Yosemite is one of the most iconic landscapes in the whole of the USA.

3 ETAPPE STAGE

4 ETAPPE STAGE

YOSEMITE **120**
LAS VEGAS **154**

LAS VEGAS **158**
PALM SPRINGS **190**

Auf der dritten Etappe überqueren wir die Sierra Nevada weiter nach Osten, biegen dann am Mono Lake ab und rollen durch das trockene Owens Valley nach Süden. Über die Bergkette der Panamint Mountains geht die Reise nun erneut nach Osten – hier ist dann endgültig der Eintritt in eine der trockensten und heißesten Gegenden der Erde geschafft: Das legendäre Death Valley zieht mit seiner eigentümlich unerbittlichen Atmosphäre jeden Besucher in seinen Bann. Bei Pahrump verlassen wir den Bundesstaat Kalifornien und rollen für eine Stippvisite ins benachbarte Nevada. Die weltberühmte Casino- und Entertainment-Stadt Las Vegas ist das Ziel dieser landschaftlich äußerst eindrücklichen Etappe.

Am Hoover-Staudamm erreichen wir den östlichsten Punkt unserer Reise. Das gigantische Bauwerk staut seit den 1930er-Jahren den Colorado River und versorgt so in einer völlig lebensfeindlichen Umgebung gleich drei Bundesstaaten mit Elektrizität und Wasser. Ab Boulder City verläuft unsere Route beinahe direkt nach Süden, bei Bullhead City haben wir wieder die Grenze nach Kalifornien erreicht und setzen die Fahrt durch die Mojave-Wüste fort. Bei Twentynine Palms verlassen wir die großen, schnurgerade verlaufenden Wüsten-Highways für einen Umweg durch den Joshua Tree National Park. Die Straße schwingt sich hier durch eine faszinierende und abwechslungsreiche Landschaft; unser Etappen-Ende erreichen wir im verträumt-mondänen Palm Springs.

On the third stage, we continue eastward across the Sierra Nevada, turning off at Mono Lake and rolling south through the parched Owens Valley. Heading across the Panamint Mountains, the journey turns eastward once more, ultimately bringing us to the entrance of one of the driest and hottest places on earth. The legendary Death Valley draws all who visit under its spell with its singularly remorseless atmosphere. We leave the state of California near Pahrump and head on into neighboring Nevada for a flying visit. The world-famous casino and entertainment city of Las Vegas is the final destination of this stage, characterized by unspeakably imposing scenery.

We reach the most easterly point of our journey at the Hoover Dam. The colossal structure has been shoring up the Colorado River since the 1930s, supplying no fewer than three states with electricity and water from utterly hostile surroundings. As of Boulder City, our route runs almost directly southward, bringing us once more to the border of California at Bullhead City, from where we continue the drive through the Mojave Desert. At Twentynine Palms, we leave the main, arrow-straight desert highway for a detour through Joshua Tree National Park. The road sweeps through a fascinating and widely diverse landscape, bringing us to the end of this stage in the wonderfully glamorous Palm Springs.

HIGHWAY 1

5 ETAPPE STAGE

PALM SPRINGS **194**
LOS ANGELES **220**

Die letzte Etappe unserer Reise durch den Westen der USA ist mit bizarren Sehenswürdigkeiten und wilden Landschaften äußerst spannend, das Tour-Finale wird darüber hinaus auf kurvenreichen Landstraßen gebührend gefeiert. Aus Palm Springs fahren wir zum Salvation Mountain, einer bunten Kunstinstallation mit religiöser Botschaft, streben dann über die wildromantischen San Jacinto Mountains in Richtung Westen. Bei Encinitas haben wir den Pazifik erreicht und setzen die Fahrt nun nach Norden fort. Vorbei an den besten Surf-Spots Südkaliforniens rollen wir zurück nach Los Angeles – das Ende der Kalifornien-Tour ist bereits in Sichtweite. Zum Abschied darf dann allerdings die herbe Angel Crest-Passstraße in den San Gabriel Mountains hinter Pasadena nicht fehlen: Erst ein Kurvenritt über die vielen Meilen einsamer Bergstraßen mit Ausblick auf die Metropole am Pazifik komplettiert die Tour.

The final stage of our journey through the west of the USA is amazing, with some bizarre sights and wild landscapes. And the tour's finale is also fittingly celebrated on some lusciously winding back roads. From Palm Springs, we drive to Salvation Mountain, a colorful art installation with a religious message, before winding our way over the ruggedly picturesque San Jacinto Mountains, heading west. We reach the Pacific at Encinitas and continue our drive northward. We head past Southern California's best surfing spots and roll on back to Los Angeles – the end of our California tour is already in sight. As a final farewell, however, we can't possible miss out the unforgiving Angel Crest mountain pass in the San Gabriel Mountains behind Pasadena. Sweeping through bend after bend along the many miles of this quiet and secluded mountain road with a view of the city on the Pacific brings the tour to a perfect close.

HIGHWAY 1 / BIG SUR

INTRO

Der Reiz Kaliforniens lässt sich vermutlich auf einen kurzen Nenner bringen: Es ist das Land am Ende des Westens, der amerikanische Traum im Konzentrat, die pure Freiheit. Völlig klischeebefreit.

Es gab eine Zeit, in der es viele Europäer sehr eilig hatten, von Zuhause wegzukommen und als Glücksritter in eigenen Diensten das Schicksal selbst in die Hand zu nehmen. Dass bei der Wahl „Amerika" auf der einen und „Russland" auf der anderen Seite am Ende die Alternative im Westen deutlich häufiger gebucht wurde, mag ein Stück weit am schlechten Wetter hinter dem Ural gelegen haben. An der stets unfassbar miserablen PR Sibiriens. Oder auch daran, dass die Menschheit erst ein paar Jahrhunderte früher aus östlicher Richtung nach Europa geritten kam, der Rückweg darum tiefenpsychologisch als Rückschritt gelten musste. Irgendwie auch egal: Wen wirklich die Wanderlust juckte, der marschierte zum Atlantik, nahm eine One-Way-Passage nach New York und verschwand in Richtung Westen.

Einmal in Fahrt ist es ganz schön schwer, anzuhalten – jeder, der gelegentlich auf Langstrecken unterwegs ist, kennt diesen Sog. Und er zieht einen immer noch weiter, auch wenn man sich längst niedergelassen hat. In Iowa, Illinois oder Oklahoma. Auf diese Weise wurde der Westen der USA zum Sehnsuchtsland aller Menschen mit Reiselust. Mit Goldrausch. Oder mit chronischer Klaustrophobie. Alles ist in Kalifornien möglich, interessanterweise muss man für diese Erkenntnis nicht einmal dort sein oder gar je dort gewesen sein. Es reicht bereits, dass man um dieses verheißungsvolle Land zwischen Rocky Mountains und Pazifik weiß.

California's appeal probably comes down to one common denominator – it's the land "out west", the essence of the American dream, of utter freedom, liberated from cliché.

There was a time when many Europeans were in a huge hurry to leave home and to take their fate into their hands as soldiers of their own fortune. When it came down to a choice between "America" on the one side and "Russia" on the other, the western alternative was by far the more popular choice, possibly due in part to the bad weather out there on the Urals – to Siberia's consistently and unbelievably miserable PR. Or maybe it was because people had ventured into Europe from the east just a few hundred years earlier and that to go back there would be seen, on a deeply psychological level, as some kind of retreat. No matter – anybody truly bitten by wanderlust made a beeline for the Atlantic; booked a one-way passage to New York and disappeared heading west.

Once you've gotten going, it's really difficult to stop again. Anyone who has occasion to take a long-distance journey knows this pull all too well. And it continues to tug at you, even long after you've settled down – in Iowa, Illinois or Oklahoma. This is how the west of the USA became the land of yearning for all those with wanderlust, with gold fever or with chronic claustrophobia. Everything is possible in California. And interestingly, people seem to be aware of this without actually being there or, indeed, ever having been there at all. It's enough simply to know that this land of promise between the Rocky Mountains and the Pacific exists. California is a way of life; an endlessly naïve belief in tomorrow. California is a state of mind – a flower-power

Kalifornien ist ein Zustand. Seelen-Firmware-Update in Flowerpower. Das Schöne an Kalifornien ist aber, dass einen dieses Land tatsächlich nicht im Stich lässt.

California is a state of mind – a flowerpower firmware update for the soul. The amazing thing about California, however, is that this land actually lives up to its reputation – still.

Kalifornien ist eine Lebenshaltung. Ein endlos naiver Glaube an den nächsten Tag. Kalifornien ist ein Zustand. Seelen-Firmware-Update in Flowerpower. Das Schöne an Kalifornien ist aber, dass einen dieses Land tatsächlich nicht im Stich lässt. Immer noch nicht. Die Realität ist farbiger, sonniger, weiter, vielfältiger, liberaler, entspannter und durchgeknallter, als man es sich irgendwo in Deutschland oder Pennsylvania ausdenken kann. Vielleicht liegt das daran, dass die Menschen Kaliforniens bereits vollständig kalifornifiziert eingewandert sind. Mit Lust auf Leben, Lust auf Erfolg und/oder individuelle Freiheit. Hier werden Stars nicht gemacht – sie werden nur noch entdeckt. Kalifornien ist wie Punk: Jeder kann es, keine Regeln!

Klar, die Goldrausch-Zeiten sind längst vorüber. Der Summer of Love hat tatsächlich nur die paar Monate gedauert. Aber das kulturelle Erbe Kaliforniens hat den Globus infiziert. Und das nicht – wie Kritiker gerne behaupten –, weil sexy Beach-Culture, die kindliche Lust auf Konsum und das kämpferisch beanspruchte Duo aus Liberalismus und Individualismus etwa in korrumpierender Manier über eine unvorbereitete Menschheit hergefallen wären, sondern weil Kalifornien etwas ungeniert ausspricht, was jeder denkt: „Hang Loose!" Kalifornien erfindet Pop. Kalifornien erfindet Skateboard, BMX und Mountainbike. Kalifornien ist Hollywood. Kalifornien ist und isst Bio-Organic-Food, buildet Bodys und wird nebenbei zum größten Hub für ganzheitliche Spiritualität weltweit: geölte Körper am Venice Beach Hand in Hand mit Ashram-Hippies aus Nordkalifornien. Und dann: Apple. Google. Kalifornien ist nicht dieser nette Klischeeort für blonde Mädels aus der Provinz, Kalifornien ist gefährlich. An Kalifornien dürfte die Zukunft nicht vorbeikommen. Eine

firmware update for the soul. The amazing thing about California, however, is that this land actually lives up to its reputation – still. The reality is more colorful, sunnier, bigger, more diverse, more liberal, more relaxed and crazier than you could ever possibly imagine in Germany or Pennsylvania. Perhaps that's because the people of California were already fully "californified" when they got here – with a lust for life, a drive for success and/or individual freedom. This is not where stars are made, simply where they are discovered. California is like punk – anyone can do it, there are no rules!

Obviously, the days of the Gold Rush are long gone and, in the end, the Summer of Love only actually lasted a couple of months. But California's cultural legacy has infected the globe. And that's not – as critics like to assert – because sexy beach culture, the childish lust for consumption and the militant pairing of liberalism and individualism somehow descended to corrupt the unprepared masses, but because California is unafraid to say what everybody was already thinking: "Hang loose!" California discovered pop music. California discovered the skateboard, the BMX and the mountain bike. California is Hollywood. California is and eats organic food, builds bodies and, along the way, has become the world's biggest hub for holistic spirituality – oiled bodies from Venice beach stand hand-in-hand with ashram hippies from northern California. And then there's Apple and Google. California is not this nice little cliché for blond girls from out in the sticks; California is

HIGHWAY 1

Sache hat Kalifornien aber aus der Vergangenheit behalten: Es ist ein Land für Unruhegeister, der Weg ist immer noch das Ziel. Hier findet das Leben auf der Straße statt, Kalifornien ist ständig in Bewegung und ein absoluter Nukleus der internationalen Car-Culture. Kaum ein anderes Land der Welt hat eine ähnliche Hingabe zu allem, was Räder hat: Fahrräder, Bikes, Autos. Kalifornische Straßen sind Tempel der Reiselust und Hochaltäre der Distanz-Eroberung. Dazu kommt eine Weite, die einen erst so richtig in schwindelerregende Trance fallen lässt. Wilde und abenteuerliche Natur. Raues Land. Sonne im Gesicht. Der Duft nach dem Staub der Wüsten, dem Salz des Pazifik, dem Grün der Wälder und der plötzlichen Erkenntnis, dass zum Fahren nicht nur die Magie der Kurven gehört, sondern auch Cinemascope-Landschaften und die ganze Atemlosigkeit des Unterwegsseins.

Genau das ist der Moment, in dem es einen als Hauptdarsteller eines Roadmovies ins gelobte Land zieht: Man müsste mal von den achtspurigen Highways im Kessel von Los Angeles auf den Mulholland Drive abbiegen, dann runter auf den Highway No. 1 an der Pazifikküste. Ortsnamen wie Songtitel: Malibu, Santa Barbara, Santa Cruz. Dann San Francisco, für eine halbe Stunde Steve McQueen sein. Eben noch Silicon Valley und plötzlich Yosemite National Park. Berge, Natur, Einsamkeit – Landschaften, die jedes Ansel Adams-Foto wie eine Steuererklärung aussehen lassen. Coffee-Stops mit Zigarette im Mundwinkel, während die Stiefelabsätze im Staub scharren. Wir sind Giganten. Und Zwerge in endloser Weite. Wir sehen zu, wie die eben grün wuchernde Wildnis von glühend heißer, verdorrter Fels-Apokalypse verschlungen wird; an der Grenze nach Nevada wissen wir schon nicht mehr, wie man das Wort „Kurve" überhaupt schreibt. Immer weiter in die Wüste und dann zwischen entsetzt und aufgerissen durch Las Vegas. Mojave Desert, Joshua Tree – ab Palm Springs kehrt das erste Mal der Glaube an ein Ende des Staubfressens wieder. Zurück in Los Angeles einfach unseren Elfer bis runter an den Strand bei Venice Beach rollen lassen. Kurz Durchatmen. Und wieder von vorne. Rewind, Repeat. *California forever.*

dangerous. There's no way the future is going to pass California by. But California has held onto one thing from the past. It is a land for restless spirits – the way is still the destination. This is where life is lived on the road. California is perpetually in motion and an absolute nucleus of international car culture. Virtually no other place in the world is quite as dedicated to anything on wheels – bicycles, motorbikes, cars. Californian roads are temples to wanderlust and the high altar of conquering long distances. It also has a vastness that sends you into an almost dizzying trance. Wild and adventurous nature, rugged landscapes, the sun on your face. The scent of the desert dust, the salt of the Pacific, the green of the forests and the sudden awareness that driving isn't all about the magic of corners and bends, but also big-screen scenery and the sheer breathlessness of travel.

This is precisely the moment when the leading actor in a road movie heads for the Promised Land. You have to turn off the eight-lane highway in the cauldron of Los Angeles onto Mulholland Drive, then onto Highway No. 1 at the Pacific coast. The place names all sound like song titles – Malibu, Santa Barbara, Santa Cruz. Then there's San Francisco and you can be Steve McQueen for half an hour. Just out of Silicon Valley and suddenly you're in Yosemite National Park. Mountains, nature, solitude – this is the kind of landscape that makes every Ansel Adams photo look like a tax return. Coffee stops cry out for a cigarette to hang loosely from the corner of your mouth, while you kick the heels of your boots through the dust. We are giants – and yet dwarves in this infinite vastness. We watch as the prolific, green wilderness is devoured by a red-hot, parched apocalypse. At the border to Nevada, we no longer even know how to spell the word "curve". We continue onwards into the desert and then, with a mixture of shock and awe, through Las Vegas. Mojave Desert, Joshua Tree – as of Palm Springs, we regain our belief that this dustfest will finally come to an end. Back in Los Angeles, we let our 911 roll down to the shore by Venice Beach. We pause for breath and start the whole thing over again. Rewind, repeat. *California forever.*

HIGHWAY 1

17 MILE DRIVE
MONTEREY

BIXBY BRIDGE

HIGHWAY 1 / BIG SUR

HIGHWAY 395

ZABRISKIE POINT

YOSEMITE
HALF DOME

HIGHWAY 1

LOS ANGELES

SALVATION MOUNTAIN

JOSHUA TREE

VALLEY OF FIRE

HIGHWAY 1 / BIG SUR

LOS ANGELES SAN FRANCISCO

835 KM • 10 STUNDEN // 520 MILES • 10 HOURS

Kalifornien. Komatöser Schlaf, hinter den wild zuckenden Augäpfeln verarbeiten sich REM-mäßig die Bilder, Gerüche und Sensationen des ersten Tags: LAX-Airport-Tower, eine Mischung aus Philippe Starck-Zitronenpresse und gelandetem Ufo. Dann der Schock, dass es dieses Kalifornien wirklich gibt, nicht nur als Action-Movie-Seifenoper-Illusion.

—

California. Emerging from comatose into REM sleep, your eyes jerk wildly as your brain processes the sights, smells and sensations of the first day. The tower of LAX Airport, a mixture between a Philippe Starck lemon squeezer and a landed UFO, then the shock that this California place really exists and isn't just an illusion created for the benefit of action movies and soap operas.

HOTELS

ACE HOTEL DOWNTOWN
929 S BROADWAY
LOS ANGELES, CA 90015
TEL. :+1 213 623 3233
WWW. ACEHOTEL.COM

THE LINE HOTEL
3515 WILSHIRE BLVD
LOS ANGELES, CA 90010
TEL. +1 213 381 7411 / 800 600 8435
WWW.THELINEHOTEL.COM

Knisternde Sommerwärme auf der Haut, Palmen winken einem blauen Himmel zu. K-ROQ im Radio des armenischen Taxifahrers, Seitenscheiben unten. Acht Spuren Asphalt und Betonplatten, die alte Starrachsen-Limousine drischt wiegend über die Bodenwellen und Schlaglöcher des Interstate-Highways. Los Angeles riecht nach Hitze, Abgas und Gegrilltem. Warmer Fahrtwind spült durch das Auto, zupft an Kleidern, Haaren und Winter-Depression. Zerschossene Kleinwagen prügeln sich um uns herum mit deutschen Premium-Limousinen, japanische Hybrid-Autos im frisch gewaschenen Klassenstreber-Look werden von riesigen Pickup-Trucks in den Schwitzkasten genommen. Röhrende Stollenreifen in Traktorgröße, Zusatzscheinwerfer, feiste Rammbügel, abgrundtief donnernder Hip-Hop-Soundtrack. Ein tätowierter Arm hängt aus dem Fenster, die Faust drischt rhythmisch aufs Türblech, H.A.T.E.-Tattoo auf den Fingerknöcheln. Willkommen im Gangland.

Links und rechts des Highways breitet sich Los Angeles aus bis an den Horizont. Pasadena im Osten, im Norden die Hollywood Hills. Flimmernder Dunst liegt über der Stadt. Los Angeles ist ein Riff aus flachen Bauten, die Downtown-Wolkenkratzer rund um den alten Stadtkern ragen in dieser endlosen Ebene aus flachen Gebäude-Würfeln und XXL-Reklametafeln auf wie eine apokalyptische Drohung. Was Dich wirklich erschüttert ist, dass diese Viermillionen-Stadt gerade einmal 230 Jahre alt ist. 1850 hatte L.A. etwas über 1600 Einwohner, im benachbarten Hollywood stand exakt ein Haus. 50 Jahre später wohnen in Los Angeles weit über 100 000, zwischen 1920 und 1930 wird mit einiger Verdoppelung innerhalb eines Jahrzehnts die erste Million geschafft.

Man hört das im Schlaf. Während Du Dich in Deinem Hotel mit aller Kraft in den Traum wirfst, ist die Stadt voller Leben. Es ist aber nicht nur das verlorene Stakkato der Polizeisirenen, das unter die dünne Schicht des Bewusstseins dringt, sondern die Aura von vier Millionen Seelen. Die Stadt der Engel.

The summer heat sizzles on your skin, palm trees wave up at a blue sky. The Armenian taxi driver is playing K-ROQ on the radio – the window rolled down. Eight lanes of asphalt and concrete slabs, the old rigid-axle sedan thrashes its way over the bumps and potholes scattered liberally all over the Interstate highway. Los Angeles smells of heat, exhaust fumes and grilled meat. Warm air washes through the car, tugging at clothes, hair and winter depression. Around us, beat-up compacts battle with German premium sedans, while freshly washed Japanese hybrids look like class nerds gripped in a headlock by enormous pickup trucks. Bellowing tractor-sized, studded tires team up with extra headlamps, fat bull bars and a booming-bass hip-hop soundtrack. A tattooed arm hangs out the window, the fist drumming rhythmically on the door panel – H.A.T.E. tattooed on the knuckles. Welcome to gangland.

Left and right of the highway, Los Angeles is spread out before you all the way to the horizon – Pasadena in the east and the Hollywood Hills to the north. A shimmering haze hangs over the city. Los Angeles is a reef of low-rise buildings, with the downtown skyscrapers of the old city center towering like an apocalyptic threat out of this endless expanse of stumpy building blocks and XXL billboards. What's truly astonishing is that this city of four million people is only 230 years old. In 1850, L.A. had a population of just over 1600, with Hollywood next door boasting exactly one house. 50 years later, there were well over 100,000, doubling a few times between 1920 and 1930 to reach its first million within a decade.

You can hear it in your sleep. While you lie in your hotel room, throwing yourself into dreamland with all your might, the city outside is full of life. However, it's not the forlorn staccato of the police sirens that forces its way beneath the thin layer of consciousness, but the aura of four million souls – the city of angels. Not until morning breaks does the city's pulse slow down somewhat. The first rays of sun reach above

Was Dich wirklich erschüttert ist, dass diese Viermillionen-Stadt gerade einmal 230 Jahre alt ist. 1850 hatte L.A. etwas über 1600 Einwohner, im benachbarten Hollywood stand exakt ein Haus.

What's truly astonishing is that this city of four million people is only 230 years old. In 1850, L.A. had a population of just over 1600, with Hollywood next door boasting exactly one house.

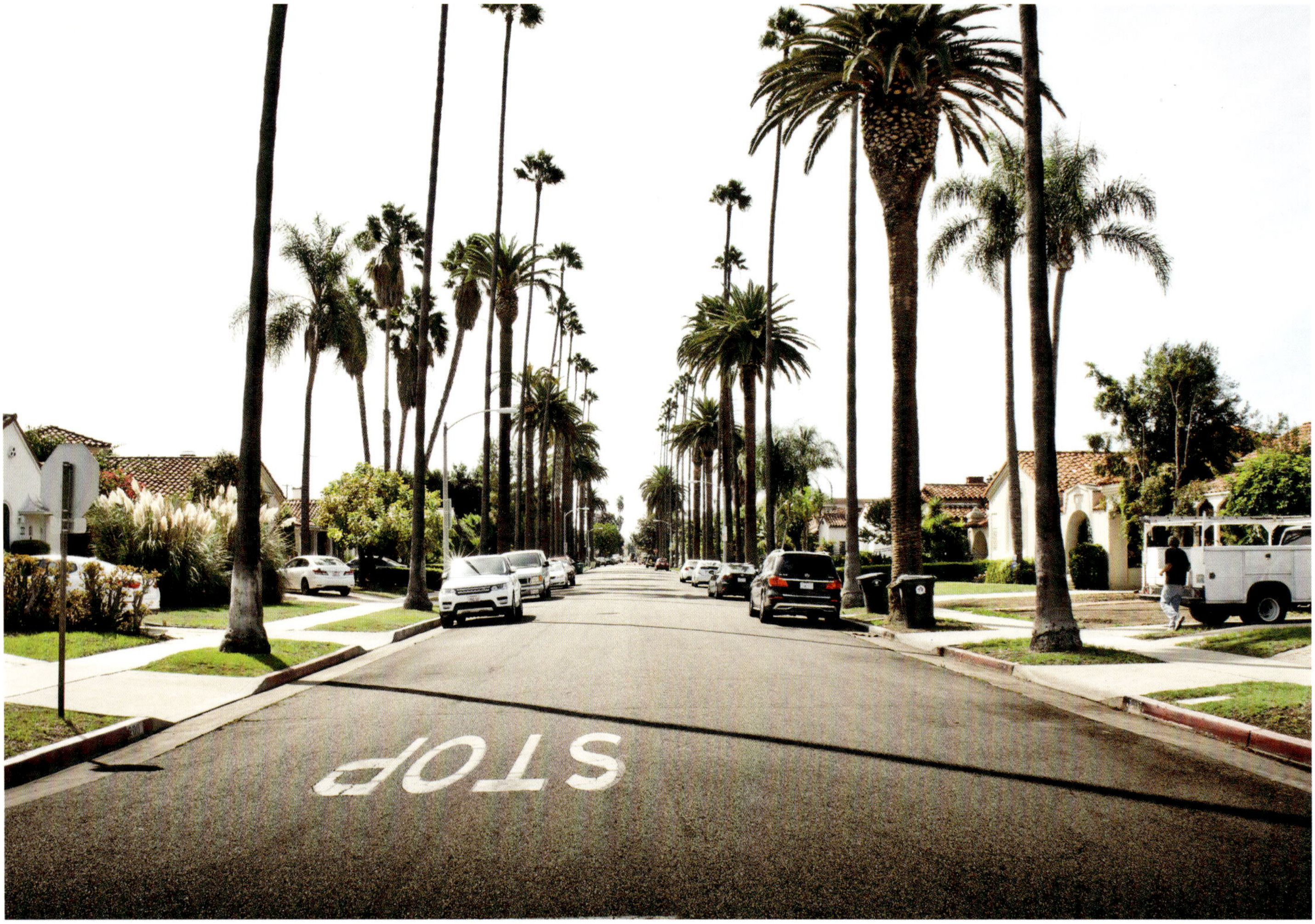
STOP

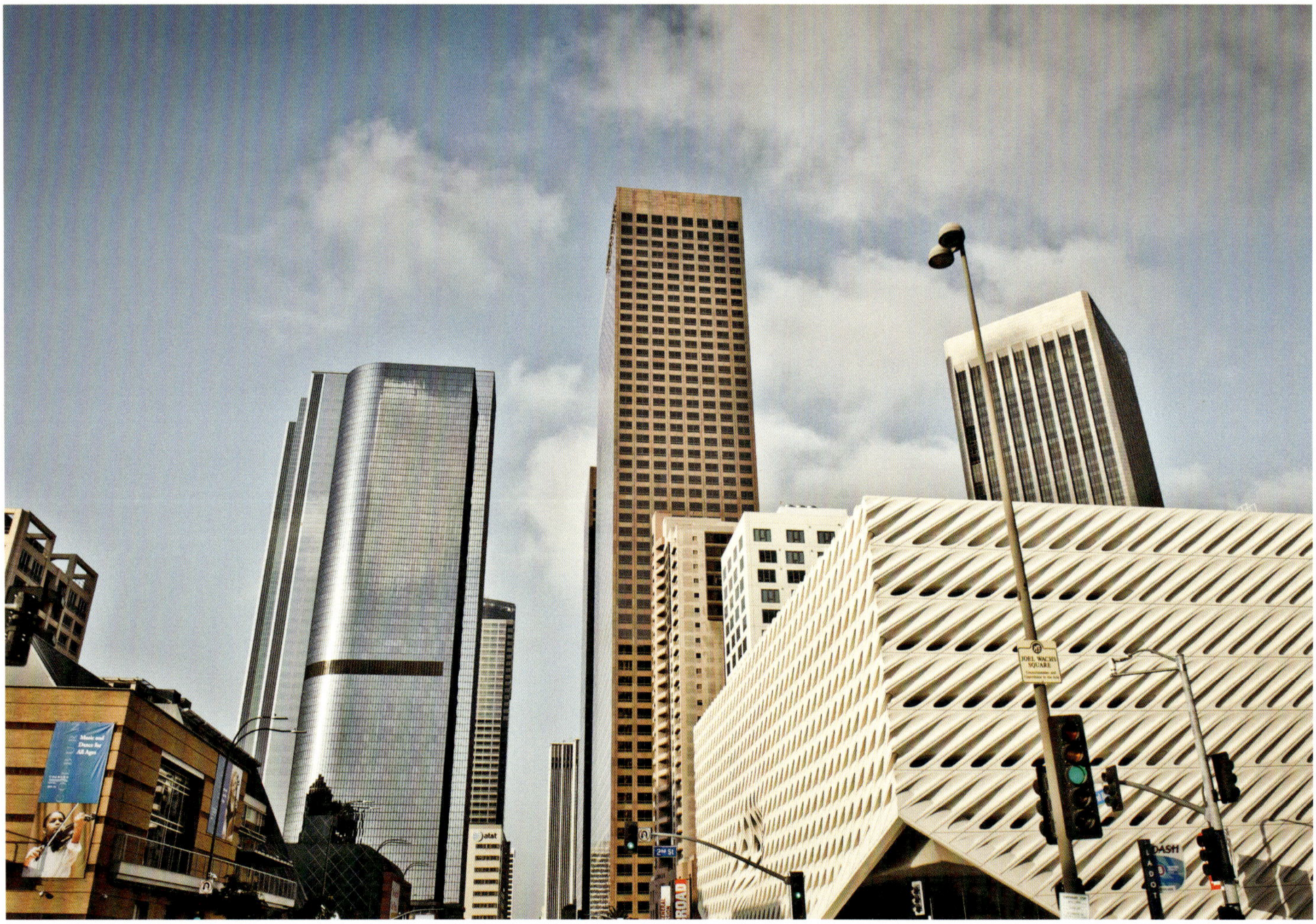
JOEL WACHS SQUARE
DASH

Erst am Morgen wird der Pulsschlag der Stadt ruhiger, die ersten Sonnenstrahlen blinken über den Bergen im Osten und machen die Palmenwipfel von Beverly Hills zu Scherenschnitten. Warmes Licht flutet durch die Straßen, Du stehst verloren am Fenster des Hotelzimmers und starrst hinaus. Los Angeles um 5 Uhr morgens wirkt wie ein schlafendes Kind.

Ganz leise rollt Dein Sportwagen dann runter zum Sunset Boulevard, vorbei an krachenden Rock'n'Roll-Legenden wie dem Roxy Club, dem Viper Room oder dem ominösen Chateau Marmont Hotel. Dann rauf zum Hollywood Boulevard. Um diese Uhrzeit sind die Gehwege mit den berühmten Sternen menschenleer, nur ein paar echte Rolling Stones gähnen neben akkurat geparkten, hoffnungslos überladenen Einkaufswagen in versifften Hauseingängen. Durch das Straßenlabyrinth in den Hügeln östlich der 101 irren wir bis zum Tahoe Drive für ein Erinnerungsfoto mit dem berühmtesten Ortsschild der Welt: Hollywood, 15 Meter hoch. Diese Touristennummer ist einem aber auch morgens um 6 Uhr peinlich, also schnell wieder rein ins Auto und runter zum Mulholland Drive. Der loopt wie eine Achterbahn durch die Berge. Unten steht gerade der „normale" Teil von Los Angeles auf, und während man mit dem Messer zwischen den Zähnen hier oben um die Ecken fegt, braucht man tatsächlich immer wieder den Panorama-Blick runter ans Meer, um überhaupt glauben zu können, dass das hier eine Straße gleich um die Ecke einer der größten Metropolen ist. Leider wird der Drive in Richtung Westen zur Schotterstraße und dann völlig unpassierbar, also muss ab dem Interstate 405 der Umweg über den Ventura Boulevard sein. Nun so schnell wie möglich auf den Mulholland Highway (nicht mit dem Boulevard verwechseln) fahren, und ob man dann über die Lost Hills Road oder den Kurvenwahnsinn im Latigo Canyon am Pazifik landet, ist völlig egal. Hauptsache PCH. Pacific Coast Highway. Number One. Hier ist das Fernweh zuhause, der Highway 1 saugt einen als Emotionswurmloch regelrecht nach Norden. Ein süßer Rausch aus Kurven

the mountains to the east and turn the tops of the Beverly Hills palm trees into silhouettes. Warm light floods through the streets; you stand lost, gazing out of the hotel room window. At five o'clock in the morning, Los Angeles somehow seems like a sleeping child.

Your sports car rolls quietly down to Sunset Boulevard, past throbbing rock & roll legends like the Roxy Club, the Viper room and the ominous Chateau Marmont Hotel. Then it's up onto Hollywood Boulevard. At this time of day, the sidewalks with the famous stars are empty, with just one or two genuine rolling stones yawning in grubby doorways next to carefully parked, hopelessly overloaded shopping carts. We wander through the labyrinthine roads in the hills east of the 101 until we reach Tahoe Drive for a snapshot with the most famous town sign in the world – Hollywood, 15 meters high. But, even at 6 o'clock in the morning, this tourist move is embarrassing, so we clamber back into the car as quickly as possible and head down onto Mulholland Drive, which loops its way through the mountains like a rollercoaster. Beneath us, the "normal" part of Los Angeles is getting up, and while we fly around the bends up here in the hills with the bit between our teeth, we really need to keep glancing at the panorama sweeping down to the ocean to actually believe that this road truly is right around the corner from such a massive metropolis. Sadly, as it heads further west, Mulholland Drive becomes a gravel road and then eventually completely unpassable, so you have to take a detour via Ventura Boulevard as of Interstate 405. You now have to get onto Mulholland Highway (not to be confused with the Boulevard) as quickly as possible. After that, it really doesn't matter whether you take the Lost Hills Road or the insane bends of Latigo Canyon to get to the Pacific, as long as you end up on PCH – the Pacific Coast Highway (Highway Number 1).

This is the true home of wanderlust. Highway 1 is like a wormhole of emotions that positively sucks you northward. It's a

MULHOLLAND DRIVE

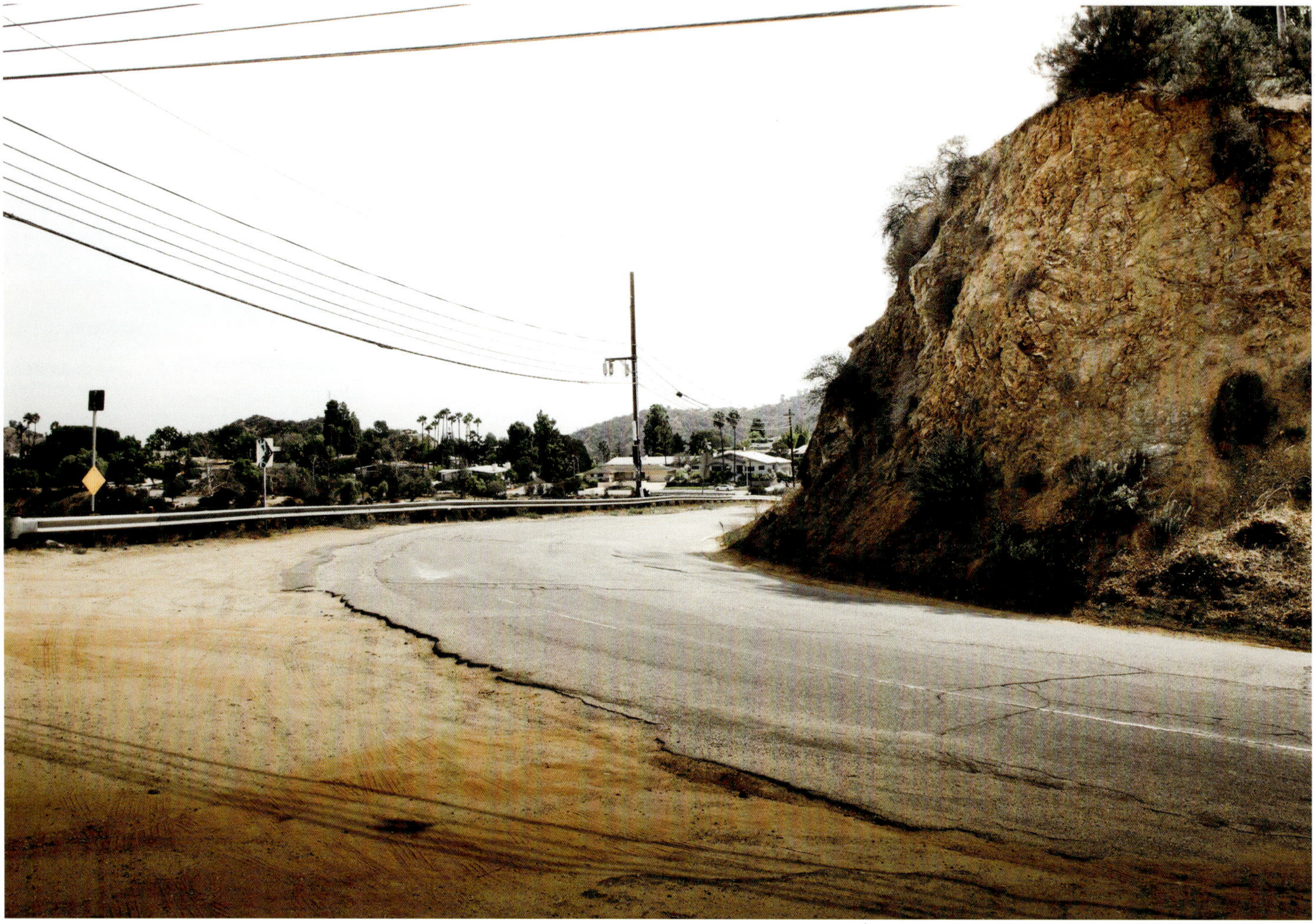

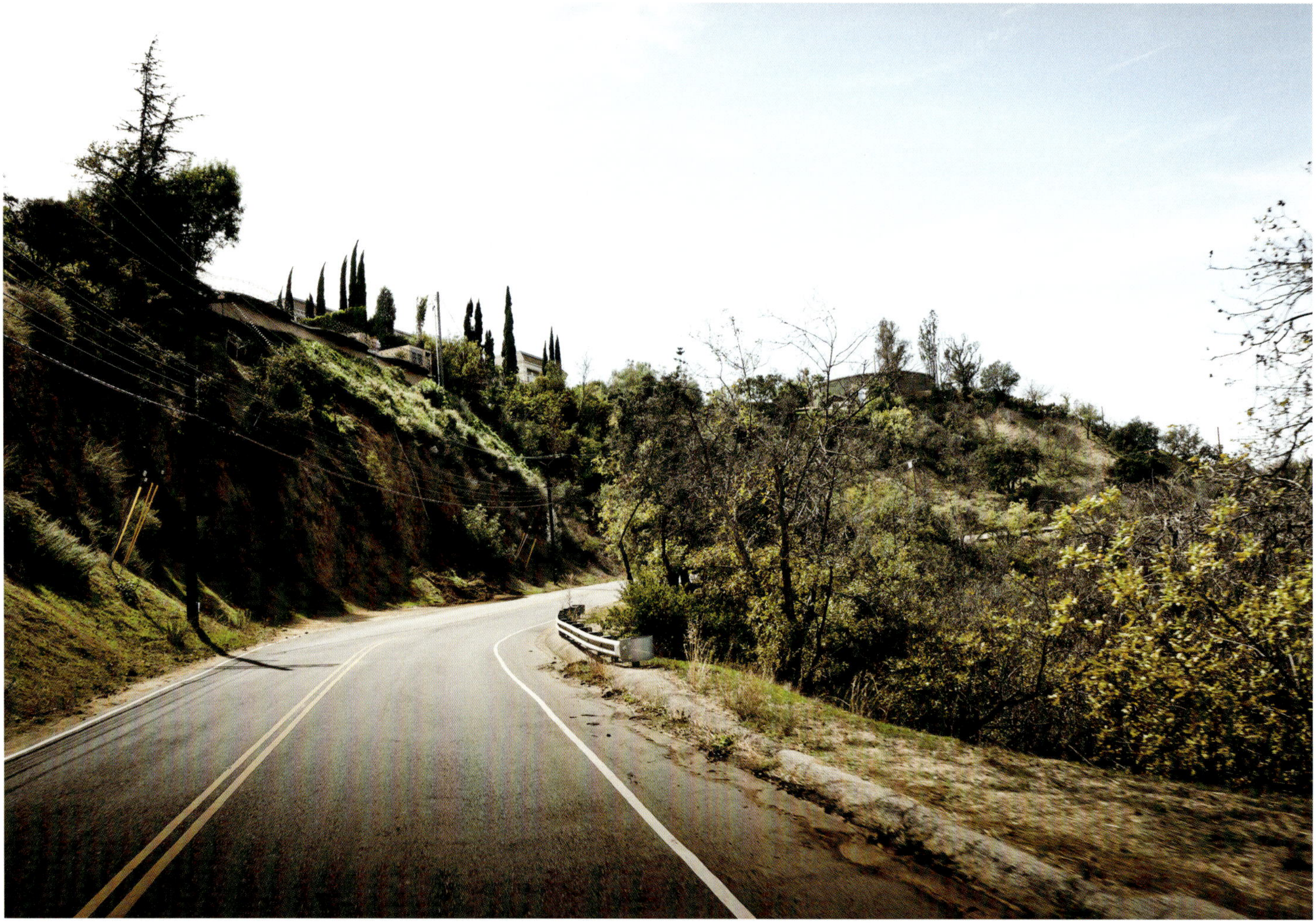

und wilden Bergen, magischer Natur und einer Bestie von gischtendem Pazifik. Hier werden Amerika-Skeptiker zu Gläubigen, die 1 auf den kleinen Schildern an der Straße zu einem verzückt wiederholten Mantra. Man liest sich die Ortsnamen vor, flüstert Ventura, lispelt Mussle Shoals, haucht Summerland und in Santa Barbara ist man eh reif für ein paar Katy Perry-Songs. Oder auch einen Kaffee und Donuts. Hauptsache Zuckerguss.

Dabei ist schon die Entstehungsgeschichte der California State Road 1 überhaupt nicht trivial: Vor dem ersten Weltkrieg musste man sich zwischen Los Angeles und San Francisco mit gebotenem Sicherheits-Abstand zum Pazifik über Bergrouten wie den Casitas-Pass schlagen. Erst mit dem Bau der Southern Pacific Coastline-Eisenbahn wurde eine Straßenroute entlang der Küste überhaupt interessant. Direkt neben der Eisenbahnlinie wurde eine unbefestigte Bau- und Versorgungsstraße mitgezogen, und genau diese Trasse mit ihren Holzbrücken über Flussmündungen oder Buchten ist die Mutter des Pacific Coast Highway. Im Süden entstehen die ersten Abschnitte, zwischen den Weltkriegen bauen Gefängnis-Insassen des Folsom Prison oder San Quentin Prison dann freiwillig die kühnen Etappenteile entlang der wilden Big Sur-Küste. Wirklich fertig wird die erste Streckenführung im Sommer 1937, seit den 1960er-Jahren heißt die gesamte Straße zwischen Dana Point im Süden und Leggett im Norden „Number 1". Mit dieser durch Menschenhand geschaffenen Tatsache ist das wilde Duo aus Pazifik und Klippen allerdings nicht ganz einverstanden: Immer wieder holen sich Erdrutsche, Erosion oder Stürme Streckenteile.

Hinter Santa Barbara wird die Straße plötzlich einsam, vor Lompoc verschwindet der Pazifik dann und taucht erst in Morro Bay wieder auf. Alles hat sich geändert, das Land ist ernst und trocken, sexy L.A. – vorbei. Die Stadt, sie ist wie klebriger Softdrink, eingetreten in plüschigen Kinoteppich. Burger-Wucht mit leichtem Desinfektionsmittel-Aroma. Außen Hitze und innen Klimaanlagen-Terror. Disney meets Botox. Während in Los Angeles selbst die Luft vibriert, kehrt sich nun alle Unruhe um.

wonderful rush of bends and wild mountains, magical nature and a beast of frothing Pacific. This is where America-skeptics become believers and where the number 1 on the small signposts along the side of the road becomes a rapturously repeated mantra. You read the place names – whisper Ventura, lisp Mussel Shoals, breathe Summerland – and in Santa Barbara, you're ready for a few Katy Perry songs, or maybe coffee and donuts. No matter, as long as it's sweet and sugary. The story behind the creation of California State Road 1, however, is far from trivial. Before the First World War, the journey between Los Angeles and San Francisco was taken a safe distance from the Pacific and involved mountain routes like the Casitas Pass. It wasn't until the construction of the Southern Pacific Coastline Railroad that any thought at all was given to the notion of a road route along the coast. An unsurfaced construction and supply road was built alongside the railroad, and exactly this track, with its wooden bridges over river estuaries and inlets, is the mother of the Pacific Coast Highway. The first sections were built in the south, then volunteer inmates from Folsom and San Quentin Penitentiaries completed the audacious stretches along the rugged Big Sur coast. The first traffic routing wasn't truly finished until summer 1937. The entire road from Dana Point in the south to Leggett in the north has been called "Number 1" since the 1960s. However, the Pacific Ocean and its cliffs are not entirely happy about this manmade interference in their shared, untamed business. Again and again, sections of the road are swept away by rockslides, erosion and storms.

North of Santa Barbara, the road suddenly becomes deserted and the Pacific disappears before Lompoc, not reappearing again until Morro Bay. Everything has changed, the land is austere and dry; sexy L.A. is gone. The city is like a sticky soft drink trodden into a plush cinema carpet; a supersized burger meal with a faint aroma of disinfectant, stifled by heat outside and freeze-dried by air-conditioning inside. It's a story of Disney meets Botox. While even the air in Los Angeles continues to vibrate, what we feel now is a

HIGHWAY 1

HIGHWAY 1

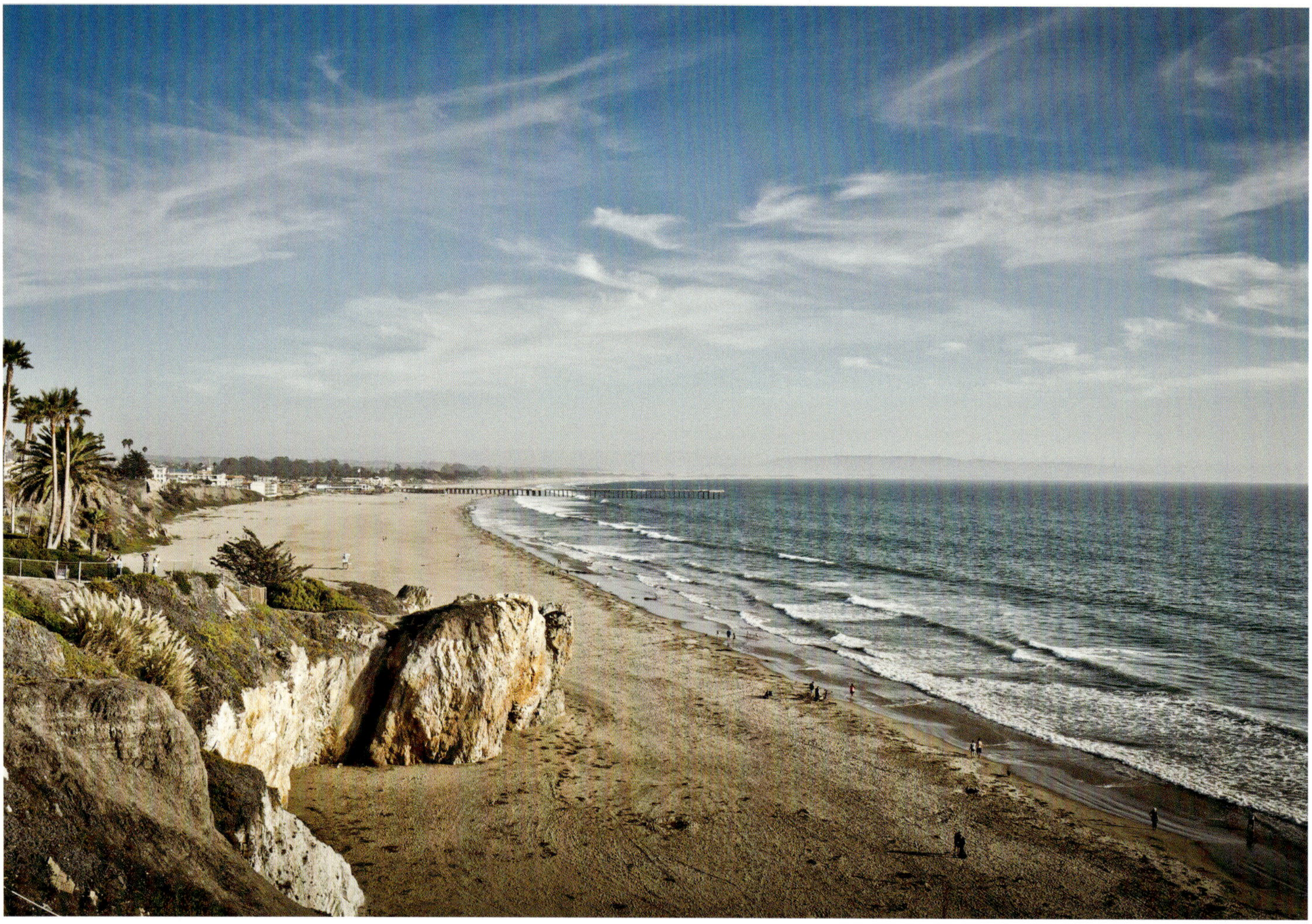

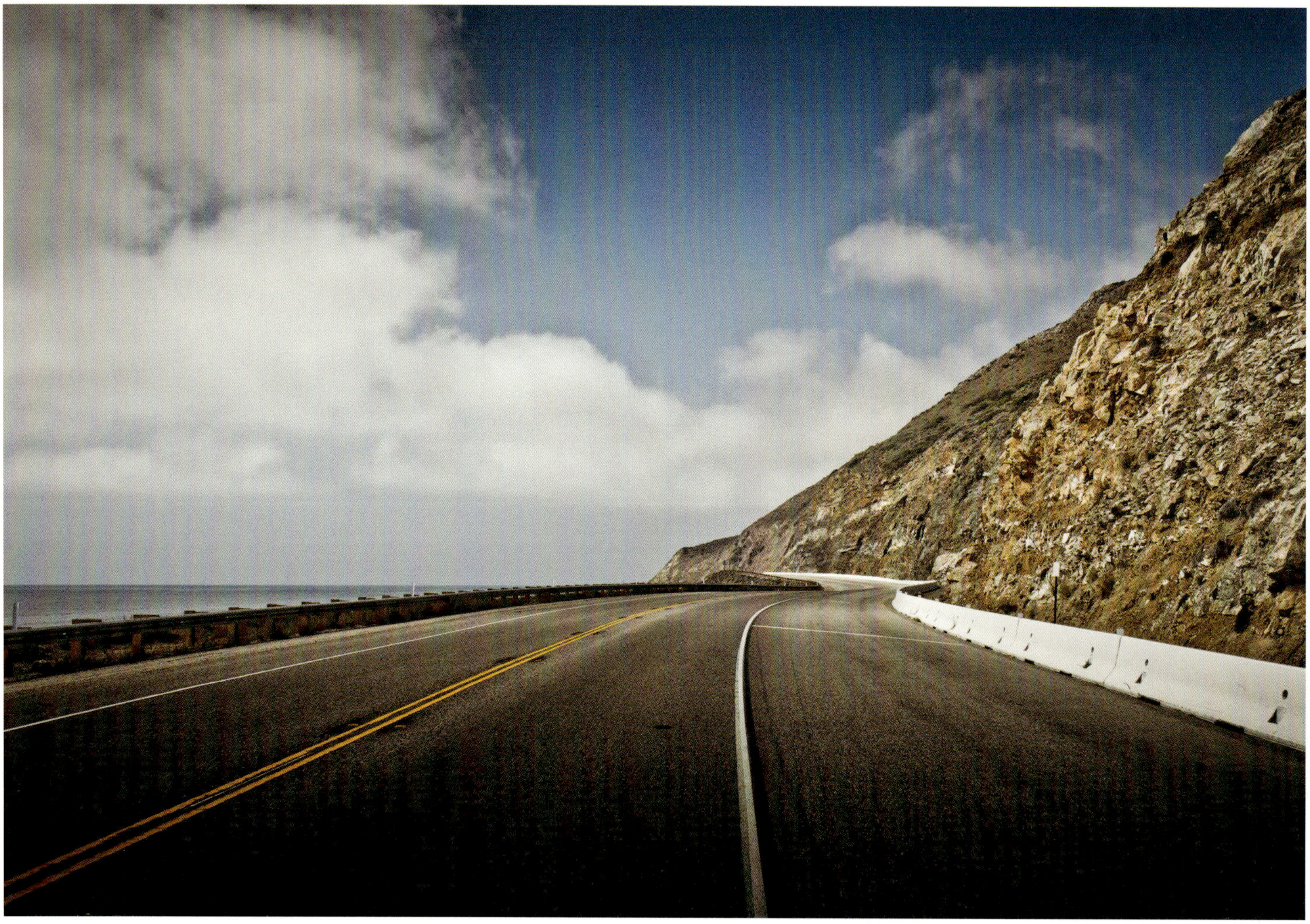

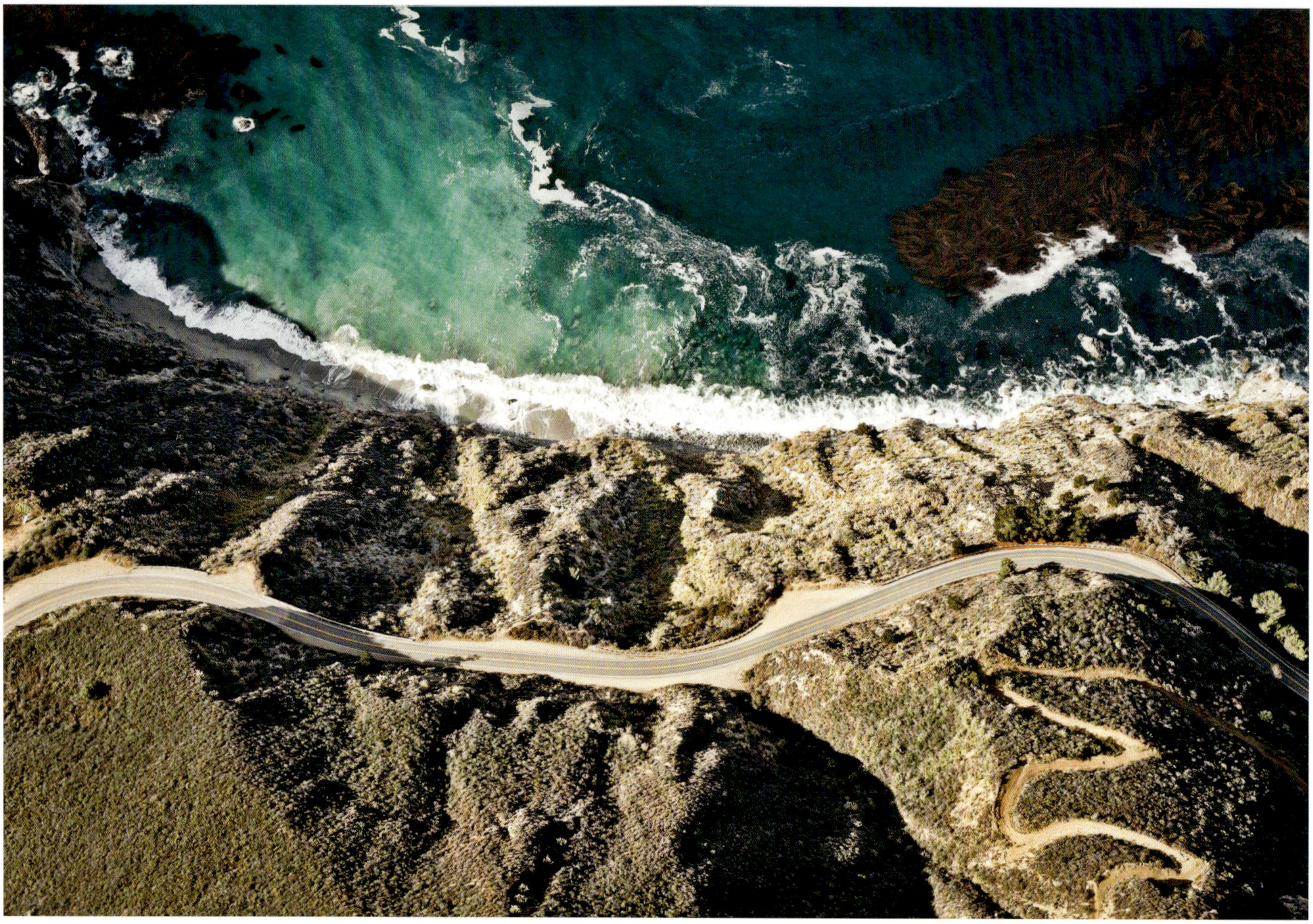

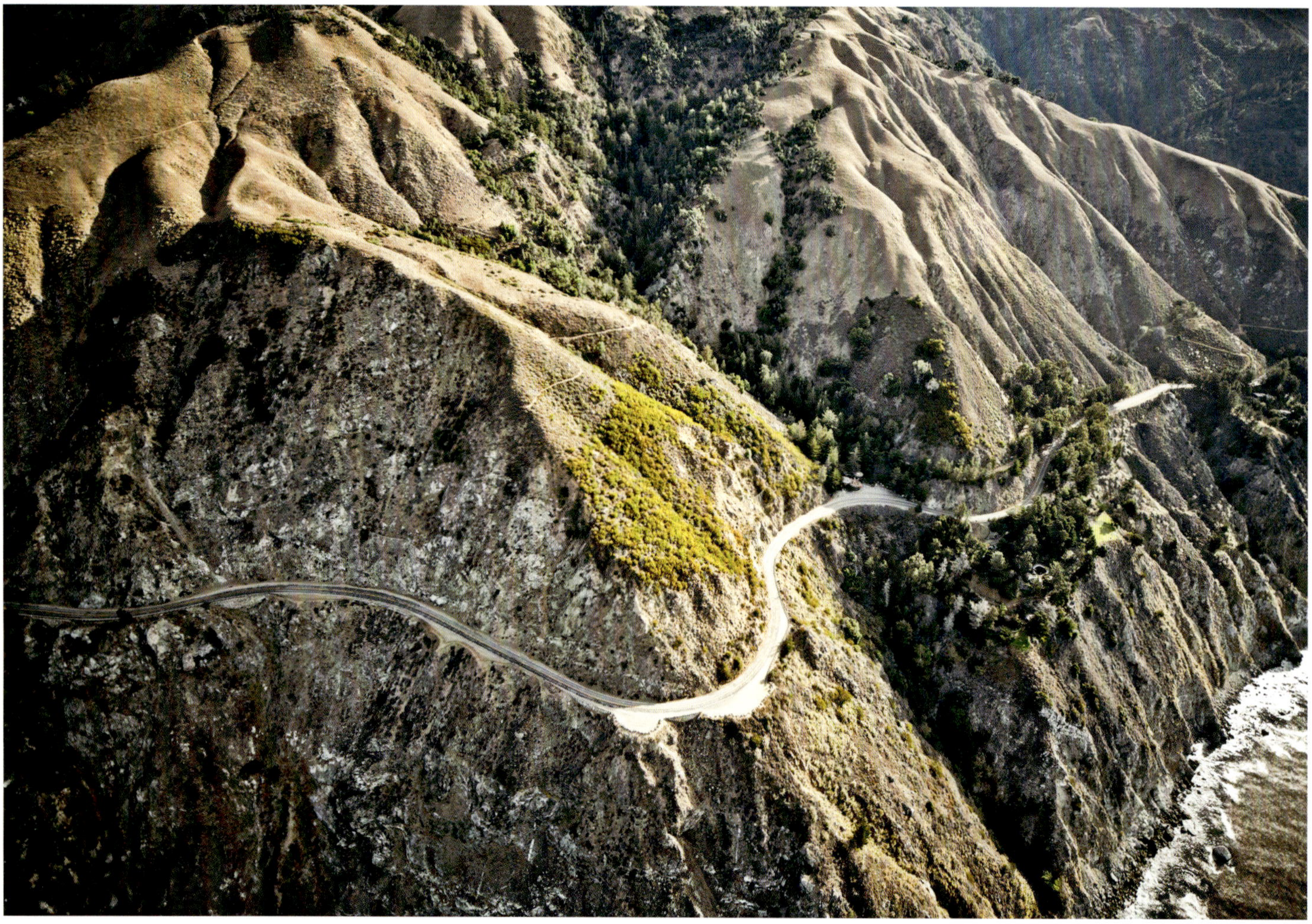

HIGHWAY 1

Willkommen in einem Kalifornien, das Du nicht erwartet hättest. Am Pier von Morro Bay spielt ein Rentner-Ehepaar mit zweistimmigem Schmelz, Stiefelabsatz-Drum-Machine und Martin-Akustikklampfe schmissige Seventies-Klassiker, derweil klaut Pele, der Pelikan, den Leuten das gegrillte Schwertfisch-Filet von den Tellern. Der ins Meer geplumpste Vulkan-Zuckerhut sagt zum Abschied kein Wort, die Straße watet nun als Cabrillo Highway durch einen dichten Teppich aus Küstenvegetation. Rechts grasen Rinder, links hypnotisiert der Pazifik: Du sitzt im Cockpit und freust Dich auf jeden Lenkeinschlag. Könntest einfach nur weinen, weil sich das Auto so sagenhaft hingebungsvoll in die Kurven wirft. Das wohldosierte An- und Abschwellen von Motorkraft, in völligem Einklang mit dem Verlauf der Topographie, der Küstenlinie, dem Wellengang. Dein Auto surft auf grünen Landwellen und das Radio hast Du schon längst ausgemacht. Wenn es vor Naturgewalt gar nicht mehr geht, legst Du einen Stopp ein, stolperst ein paar Schritte ins Klippengras und hältst das Gesicht mit geschlossenen Augen in den Wind. Sprachlos machende Schönheit in vollkommener Überdosierung. Das muss man verkraften.

Bei Big Sur hat man sich aber schon beinahe an dieses wilde, milde Land gewöhnt, schickt einen Schnappschuss von der Bixby Bridge nach Hause: Selfie mit Sportwagen-Legende, lachend. Ab dann jagen sich andere Legenden: Bei Carmel lockt der mautpflichtige 17 Mile Drive, in Monterey müsste man sich eigentlich die Cannery Row ansehen, aber da John Steinbeck gerüchtehalber eh mit James Dean (der es mit seinem Porsche 550 Spyder nie zur Rennstrecke hinten in der Lagune geschafft hat) in den Bergen bei Salinas abhängt, kann man sich den Besuch auf der Touristenmeile vielleicht auch sparen. In Moss Landing auf einem Walbeobachtungs-Schiff anheuern? Oder in Santa Cruz, am anderen Ende der Monterey Bay, für immer aussteigen und seine Tage als Surfer beschließen? Natürlich nicht. Die Straße zieht weiter, wir springen auf. Rollen durch Half Moon Bay und Pacifica – dann sind da diese gigantischen Brückenpfeiler in Rostschutz-Rot. Golden Gate. Glühend im letzten Licht des Tages.

sense of calm returning. Welcome to a California you didn't expect. At the Morro Bay Pier an elderly couple sings catchy seventies classics in two-part harmony, playing a stompbox drum machine and Martin acoustic guitar, while Pele the pelican steals grilled swordfish fillet from diners' plates. The Morro Rock volcanic plug poking out of the ocean offers no words of farewell. The Cabrillo Highway lies ahead, winding its way through a thick carpet of coastal vegetation. Grazing cattle to the right and, to the left, the hypnotic expanse of the Pacific Ocean – you sit in the cockpit, enjoying every turn of the steering wheel. You could weep as the car throws itself into each and every bend with such phenomenal devotion. You sense the finely metered ebb and flow of the engine's power, completely in harmony with the topography, the coastline, the waves. The car is surfing on a green swell of land. You turned off the radio miles back. When you can simply no longer handle the sheer force of nature, you take a break, stumble through the grass on the clifftops and hold your face into the wind, with your eyes closed. This overdose of utter beauty leaves you speechless – you have no choice but to absorb it.

By Big Sur, you've almost become accustomed to this wild, gentle land – you send home a snapshot of the Bixby Bridge, a smiling selfie alongside the legendary sports car. But this is when the legends start flowing one after the other. Near Carmel, you're enticed by the 17 Mile Drive toll road, and you simply have to see Monterey's Cannery Row. But then again, maybe you can spare yourself the visit to the tourist hotspot because, in the mountains near Salinas, John Steinbeck is allegedly hanging out with James Dean (who never made it to the racetrack with his Porsche 550 Spyder). And what about chartering a whale-watching boat in Moss Landing? Or leaving the rat race forever in Santa Cruz at the other end of Monterey Bay, and living out your days as a surfer dude? Of course not. The road is calling and we forge ahead – rolling through Half Moon Bay and Pacifica. Then, in the last light of the day, we see these enormous bridge pylons glowing in rust-proof red – the Golden Gate.

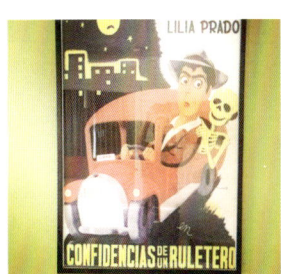

HOTELS

AGAVE INN
3222 STATE ST
SANTA BARBARA, CA 93105,
TEL. +1 805 687 6009
WWW.AGAVEINNSB.COM

COLONIAL TERRACE INN
SAN ANTONIO AVE
CARMEL-BY-THE-SEA, CA 93921
TEL. +1 831 624 2741

RESTAURANT

SAMA SAMA KITCHEN
1208 STATE ST
SANTA BARBARA, CA 93101
TEL. +1 805 965 4566
WWW.SAMASAMAKITCHEN.COM

BIG SUR BAKERY
47540 CA-1
BIG SUR, CA 93920
TEL. +1 831 667 0520
WWW.BIGSURBAKERY.COM

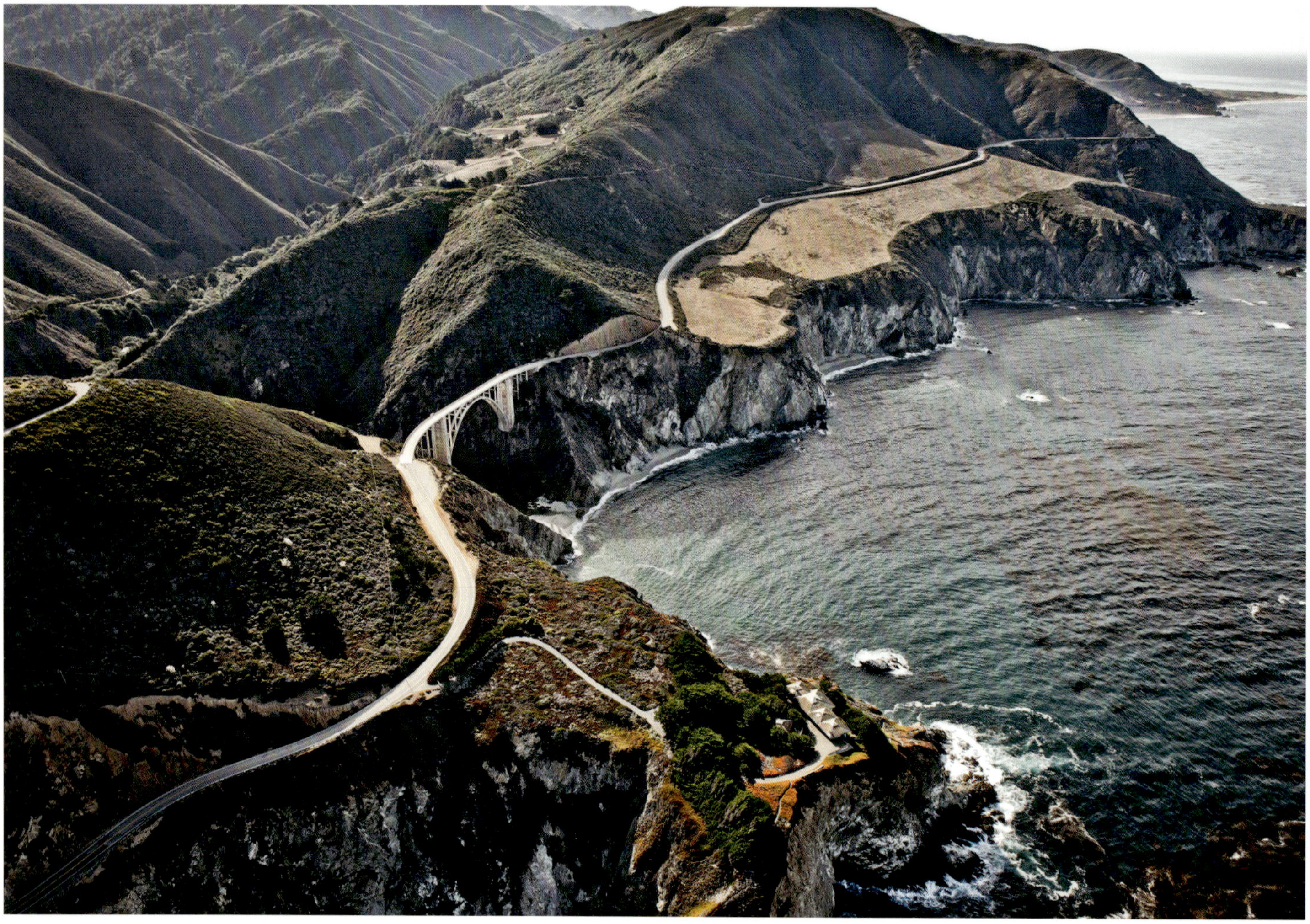

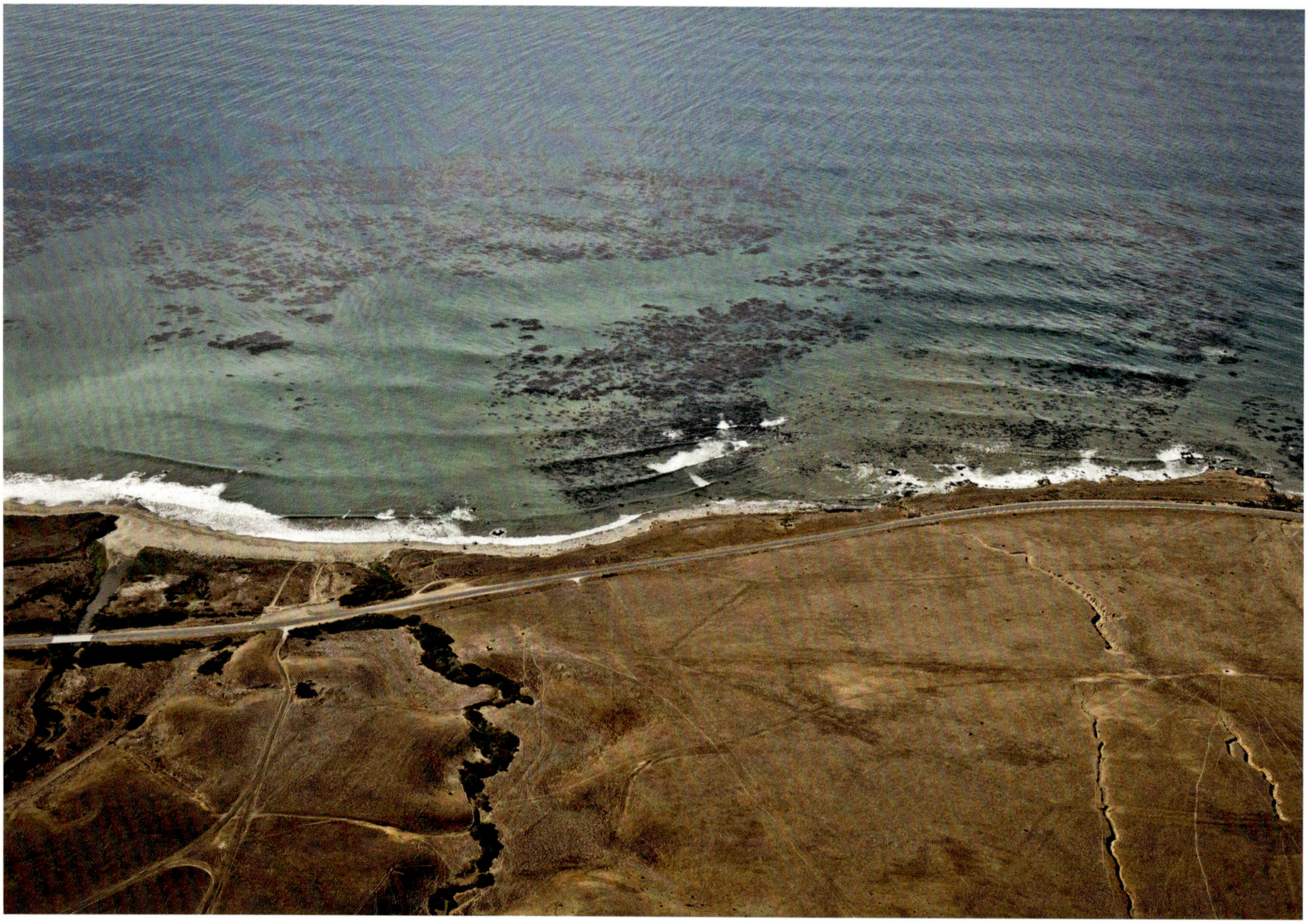

BIXBY BRIDGE

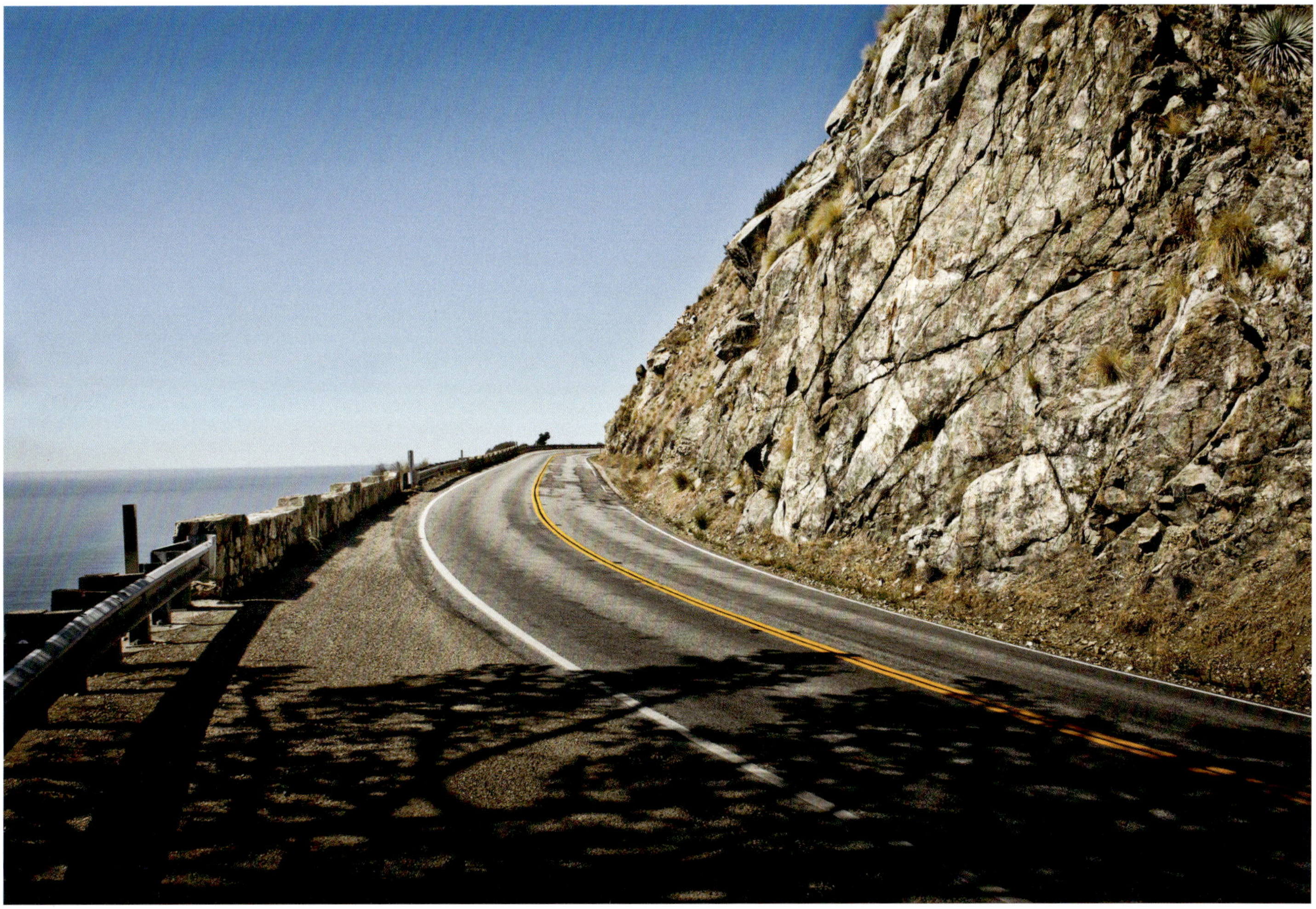

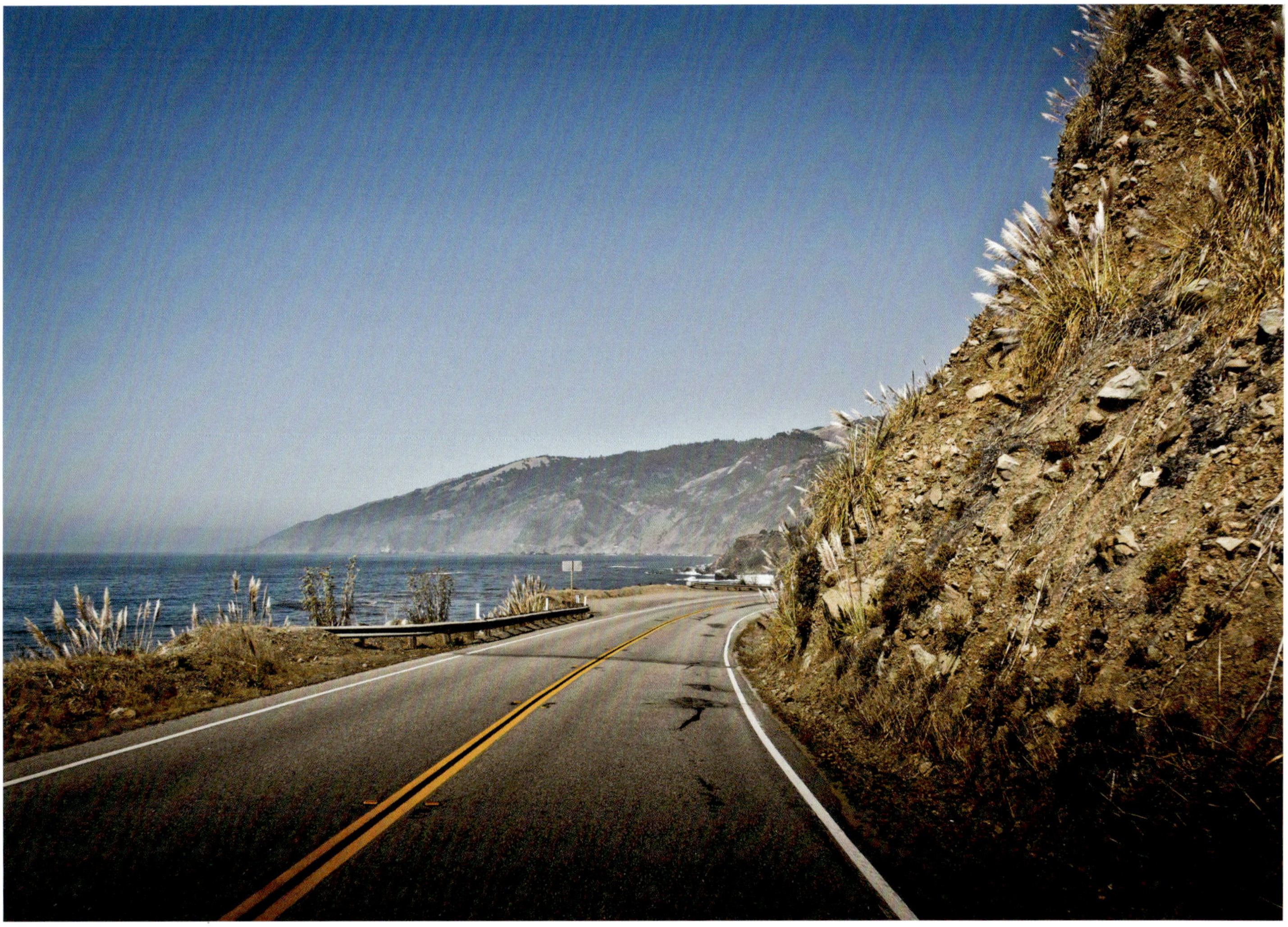

17 MILE DRIVE

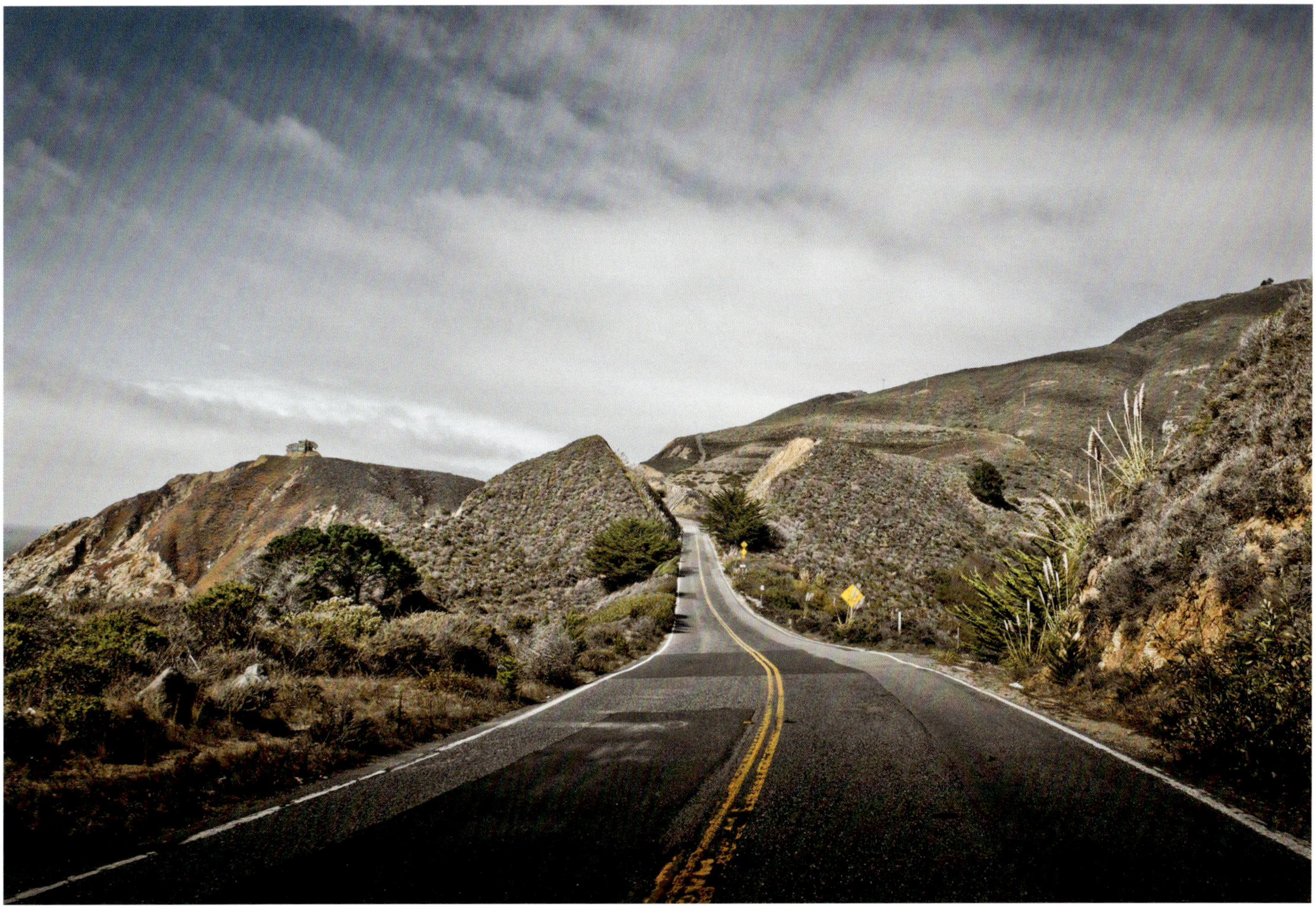

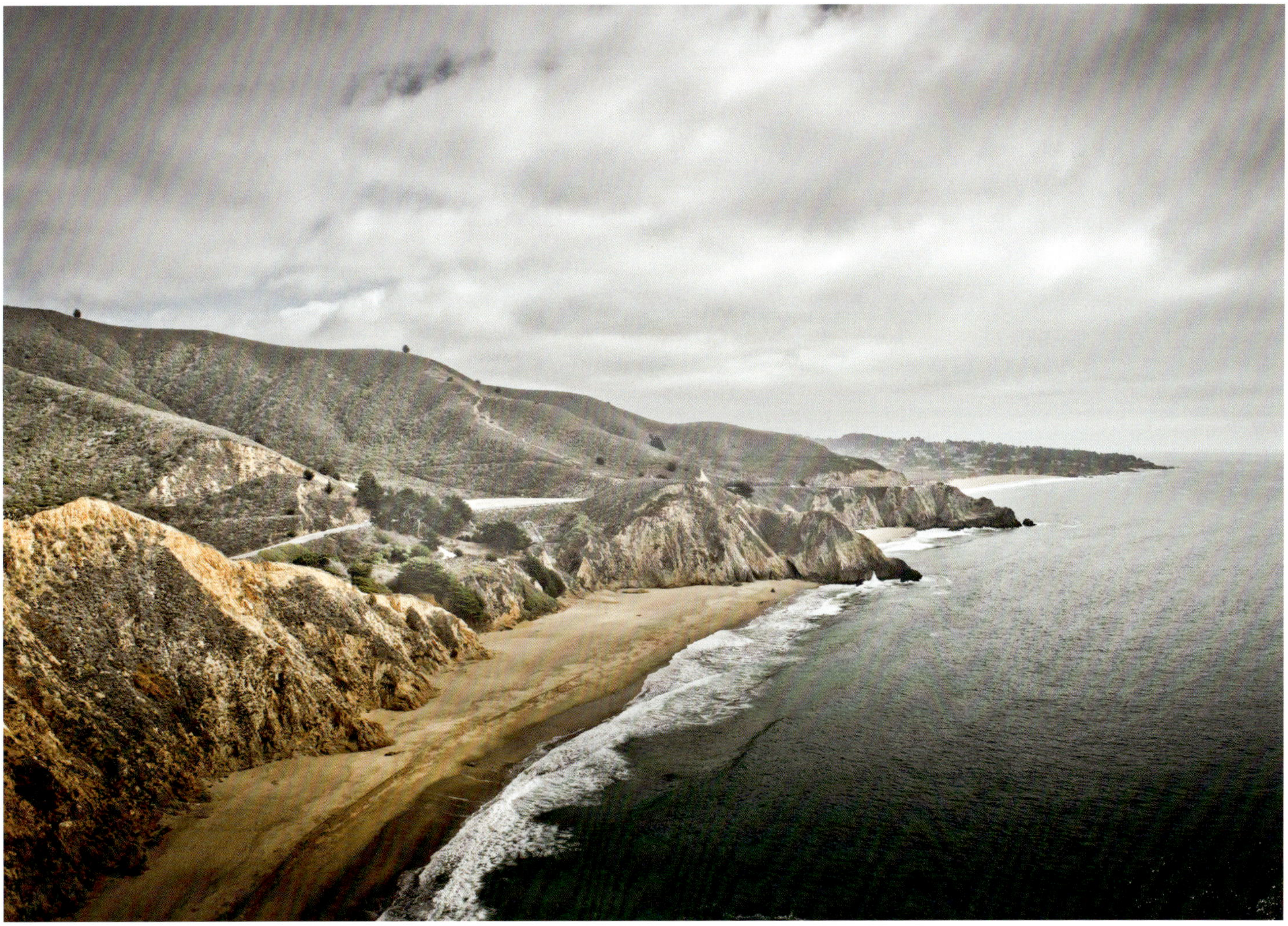

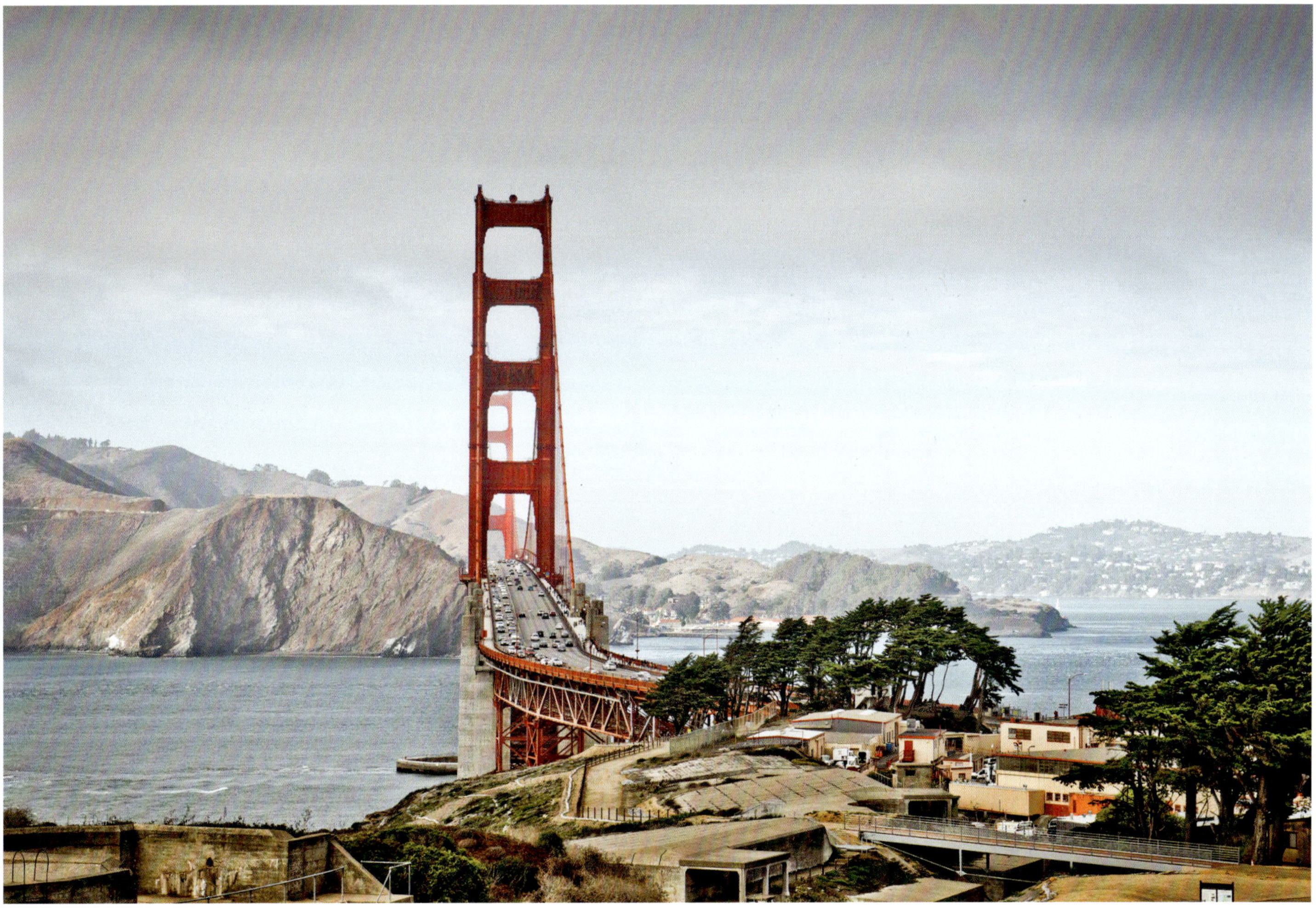

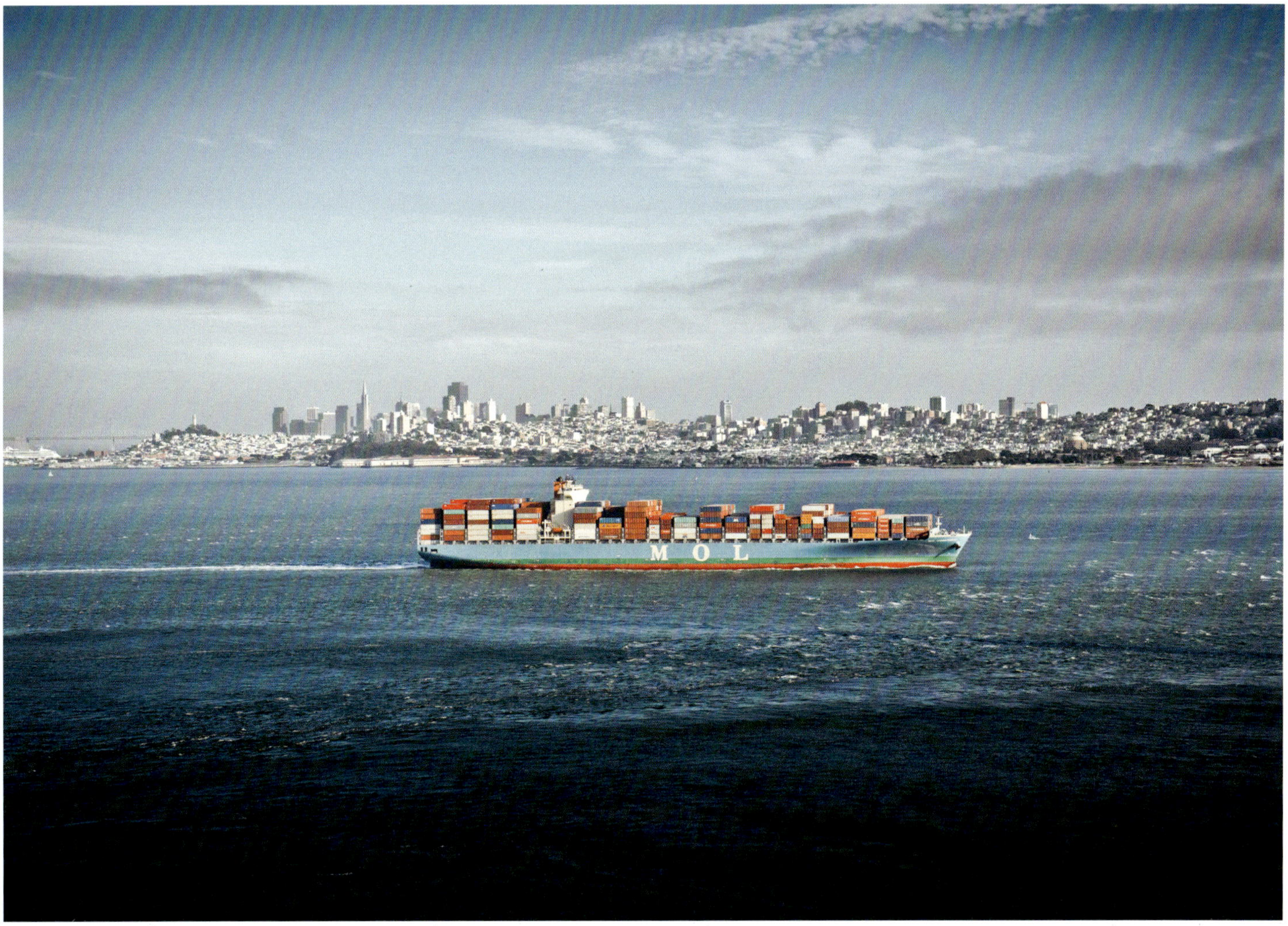
M O L

LOS ANGELES SAN FRANCISCO

Die Autostadt Los Angeles will ausgiebig erkundet werden. Zwischen Manhattan Beach und Pasadena, Long Beach und Beverly Hills ist ein Auto ideales Fortbewegungsmittel, um der energiegeladenen Metropolregion ganz nahe zu kommen. Am Ende verlassen wir das Stadtgebiet über die Hollywood Hills und den Mulholland Drive nach Norden, landen dann aber bei Malibu wieder an der Pazifikküste. Der PCH, Pacific Coast Highway, ist nun für die nächsten Stunden unsere Sehnsuchtsstraße, zwischen Bergen und Meer fahren wir nach Norden. Dabei sind nicht nur die Fischer- und Surfer-Städte am Meer, die immer noch den legendär coolen California-Lifestyle ausstrahlen eine Reise wert, sondern auch die Straße an sich: Spektakuläre Natur, grandiose Streckenführung – der Highway Number 1 gehört zweifelsfrei zu den schönsten Straßen der Welt. Nach einer intensiven Begegnung mit den belebten und spannenden Städten rund um die Monterey Bay ziehen wir weiter über die Half Moon Bay nach Norden und erreichen mit San Francisco das erste Etappenziel.

—

The auto city of Los Angeles is crying out to be explored. From Manhattan Beach to Pasadena, Long Beach to Beverly Hills, a car is the ideal means of transportation for getting up close and personal with this energy-charged metropolis. At the end, we leave the city via the Hollywood Hills and Mulholland Drive heading north, landing back at the Pacific coast near Malibu. The PCH, Pacific Coast Highway, is now the road of our desire, taking us northward between mountain and ocean. It's not just the fishing and surfing towns along the coast that make this journey worthwhile, still radiating that legendary, cool Californian lifestyle, but the road in and of itself. Spectacular nature, amazing twists and turns – Highway No. 1 is without doubt one of the most beautiful roads in the world. Following an intense encounter with the vibrant and exciting towns around Monterey Bay, we continue north via Half Moon Bay, reaching the end of our first stage in San Francisco.

835 KM • 10 STUNDEN // 520 MILES • 10 HOURS

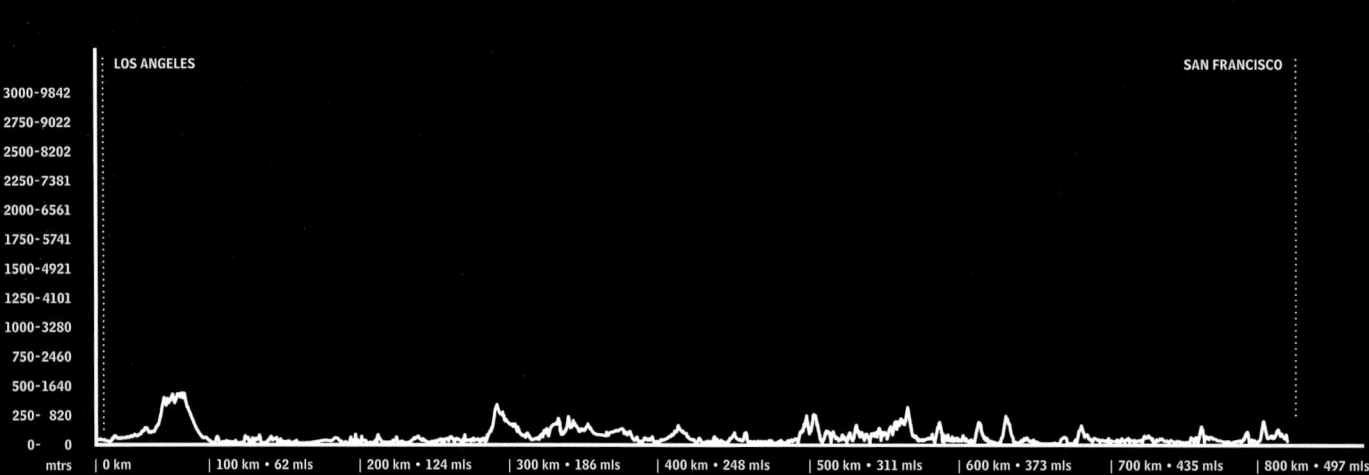

SAN FRANCISCO YOSEMITE

310 KM • 4 STUNDEN // 192 MILES • 4 HOURS

Wie hypnotisiert geradeaus fahren. Die Magie der letzten 450 Meilen hat Dich in eine Parallelwelt versetzt, vor Deinem inneren Auge spult sich immer noch diese Küstenstraße ab: schroffe Klippen, ganz Amerika stürzt hier in den Pazifik, ein schmales Asphaltband tastet sich durch eine unfassbar majestätische Landschaft, die Luft ist mit einem glasigen Dunst aus salzigem Nebel erfüllt.

—

Keep driving straight ahead – as if hypnotized. The magic of the last 450 miles has shifted into a parallel world. This coastal road is still playing out in your mind's eye – rugged cliffs, where all of America comes to a shuddering halt and tumbles into the Pacific, and where a narrow band of asphalt feels its way through an unfathomably majestic landscape, the air filled with a glassy haze of salty mist.

HOTELS

THE AHWAHNEE
1 AHWAHNEE DRIVE
YOSEMITE NATIONAL PARK
CA 95389
TEL. +1 801 559 4884
WWW.YOSEMITEPARK.COM/
THE-AHWAHNEE.ASPX

Und jetzt, in der Stunde zwischen spätem Nachmittag und Abend, hat sich eine zähe Trance in Deinen Synapsen festgesetzt. Du bist das Auto, Du bist Bewegung, Du bist die Straße. Anhalten beinahe unmöglich, ein Stopp würde sich jetzt wie Verrat anfühlen. Nach endlosen Meilen der Menschenleere unten an der Küste wirken die Stadtrandgebiete von San Francisco wie ein Schock. Das Auto segelt durch ein Spalier von flachen Häuserzeilen zwischen Sunset District und Golden Gate Heights, Pastellfarben, nie mehr als zwei Stockwerke. Meile um Meile. Dann plötzlich die mehrspurigen Betonrampen durch den Golden Gate Park, ein Hechtsprung auf die 101 – und da vorne ist sie. Die Brücke aller Brücken. Golden Gate. Das Tor nach Kalifornien. Die Abendsonne lässt das Rot der Seile und Pfeiler leuchten, sechs Spuren Asphalt streben himmelhoch über die Meerenge zwischen San Francisco und Marin County. Gleich hinter der Brücke geht es raus auf die Conzelman Road und nach ein paar Kehren strandet das Auto am Vista Point hoch über dem Meer. An dem kleinen Parkplatz dort ist irgendwie immer eine Lücke frei – und dann taumelst Du ein paar Meter den Hang hinauf, fällst ins Gras und schaust verzückt über die Bucht. San Francisco, wie ein Traum. Langsam beginnen die Wolkenkratzer der Stadt zu leuchten, die Abendsonne spiegelt sich tiefrot in den Glasfassaden. Eine steife Brise weht über die Küstenlinie, weit unten im mahlenden Gezeitenstrom retten sich kleine, weiße Segel-Dreiecke vor der Dunkelheit in den Hafen. Dann brennt das gesamte Universum in Dunkelrot, wird trüber, stumpfer und immer fahler, mit Einbruch der Dunkelheit steigt San Francisco wie ein glitzerndes Ufo aus der Nacht. Zurück zum Auto, hinunter zur Brücke, den Ruf der immer weiter in Richtung Norden fließenden State Road 1 überhören wir – im Osten wartet ein neues Land auf Entdeckung.

Man könnte jetzt drei Dinge tun: Erstens dem inneren Steve McQueen Auslauf geben und im Bullitt-Style über die steilen Hügelstraßen der Stadt donnern. Das macht auch bei gesetzeskonformem Innenstadt-Tempo noch einigermaßen Spaß; schließlich sind die Rampen teilweise derartig steil und die betonierten Wasserrinnen an den Querstraßen so tief, dass sich eine Stadtrundfahrt auch

And now, in the hour between late afternoon and evening, a tenacious trance has set into your synapses. You are the car, you are movement, you are the road. Stopping would be all but impossible; it would feel like a betrayal. After endless miles of solitude down by the coast, the outer edges of San Francisco are something of a shock. The car sails through low rows of houses, standing like a guard of honor between Sunset District and Golden Gate Heights, all in pastel colors, none of them higher than two stories – mile after mile. Then suddenly we're on the multi-lane concrete ramps through the Golden Gate Park, diving down onto the 101, and there it is – the bridge of all bridges – Golden Gate, the gate to California. The evening sun sets aglow the red of the cables and pylons. Six lanes of asphalt soar into the sky over the straits between San Francisco and Marin County. Right after the bridge, we turn onto Conzelman Road and, after a few bends, the car comes to a halt high above the ocean at Vista Point. Somehow, there's always a space at the little parking lot – and you stagger a few meters up the hillside, collapse into the grass and gaze in amazement over the bay – San Francisco lies before you like a dream. Slowly, the city's skyscrapers start to glow, the evening sun reflected deep red in their glass facades. A stiff breeze blows along the coastline. Way down in the tidal flow, small, white triangles of sail flee the impending darkness for the shelter of the harbor. The whole universe blazes dark red, then fades, becoming duller and paler. As darkness arrives, San Francisco rises into the night like a glittering UFO. We climb back into the car, head down to the bridge, ignoring the call of State Road 1 as it continues on its way northward – there's a whole new land to the east awaiting discovery.

There are three things you could do now – first, vent your inner Steve McQueen and thunder along the hilly streets Bullitt-style. Even at city speed limits it's still pretty good fun; some of the inclines are so steep and the concrete gutters on the intersections so deep that even a low-speed city drive is quite an experience. Incidentally, feel free to leave out the famous Lombard Street with its tight serpentines. Its entertainment value is barely more than that of a

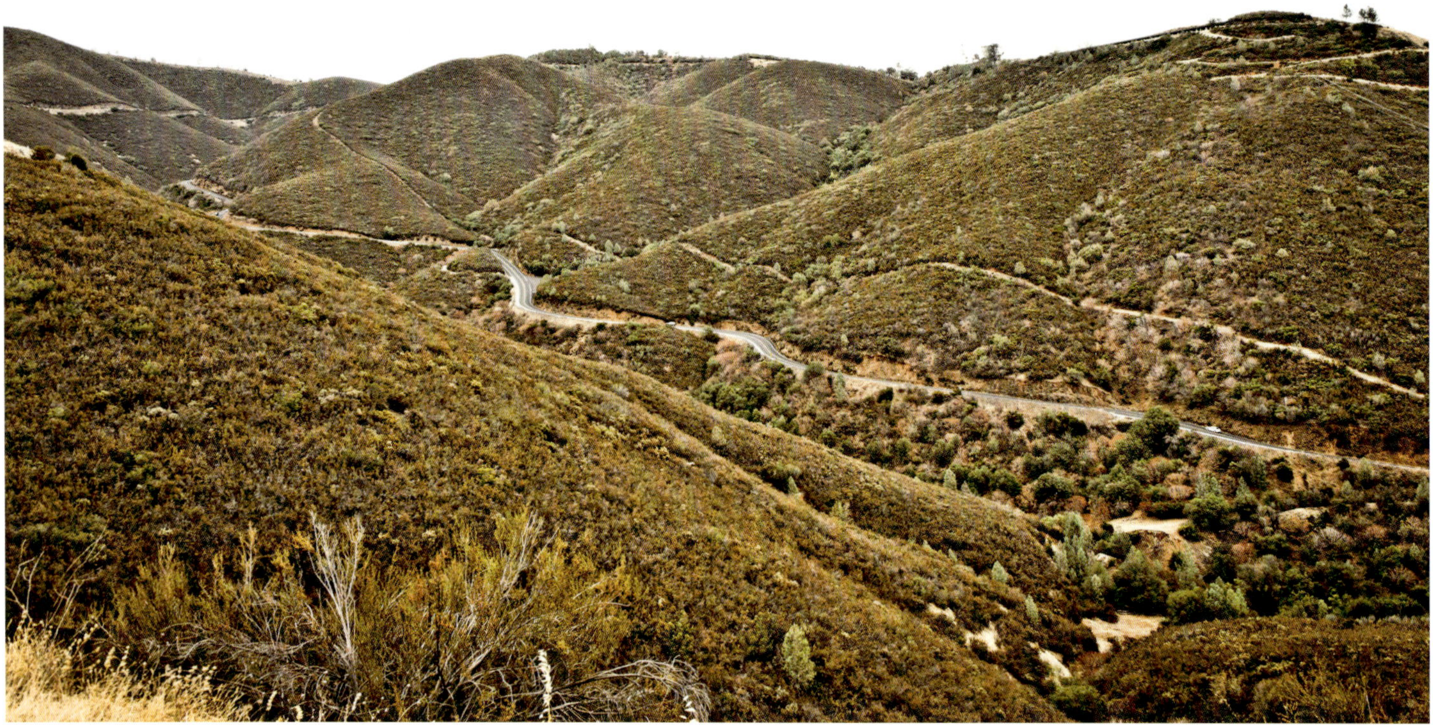

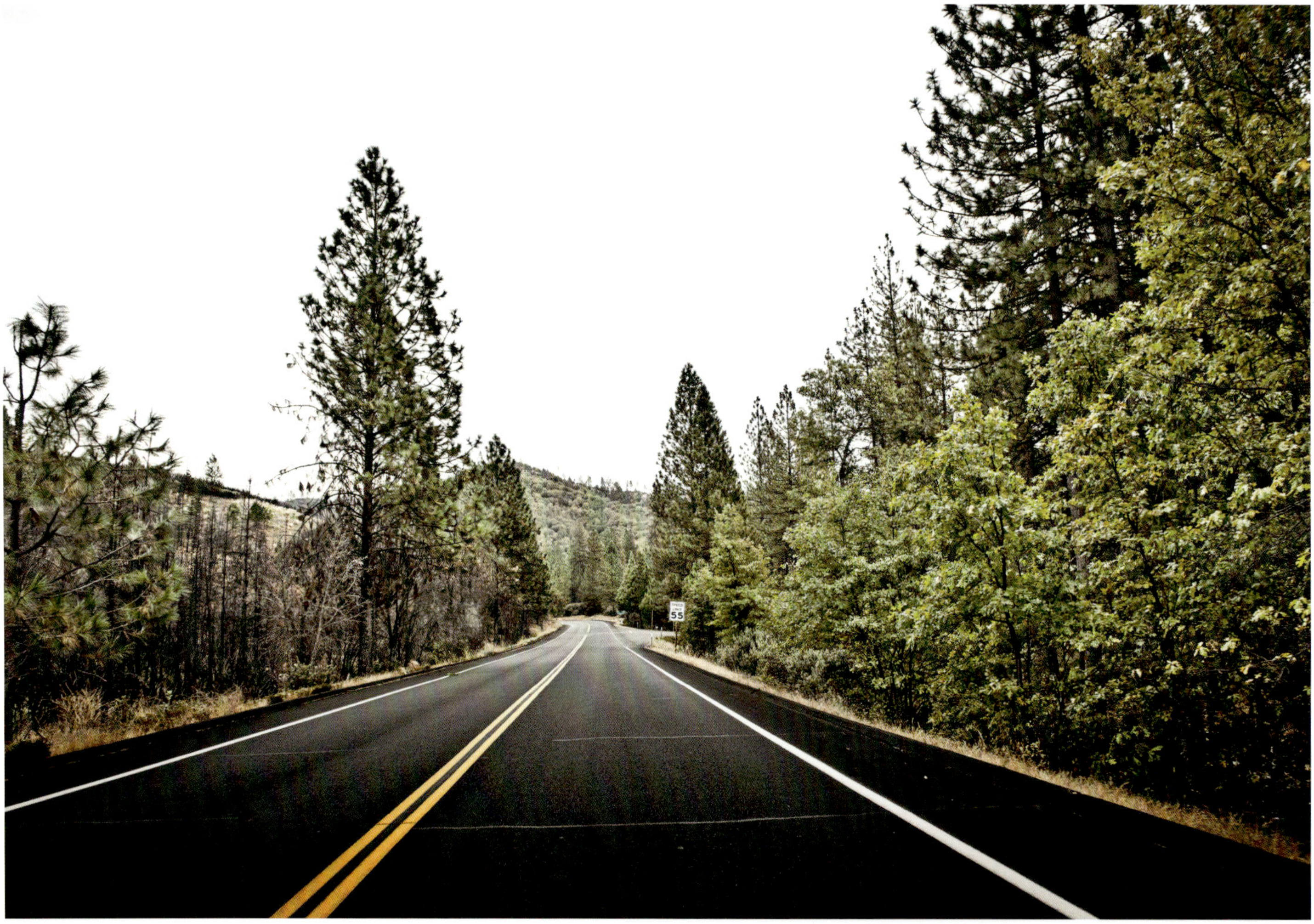
55

mit gebremstem Schaum ziemlich heftig anfühlt. Die berühmte Lombard Street mit ihren engen Serpentinen darf dabei übrigens getrost ausgelassen werden, ihr Unterhaltungswert geht über den einer reinen Kuriosität kaum hinaus. Zweitens gäbe es die Möglichkeit zum Besuch der High Tech-Zentralen im Silicon Valley. Die Gegend ist allerdings so industriell, steril und langweilig, dass nur eingefleischte Apple- oder Google-Fans an den entsprechenden Adressen in Cupertino oder Mountain View eine ehrfürchtige Gänsehaut bekommen. Abgehakt.

Bleibt die dritte Option: zwei Tage High Voltage-Sightseeing in San Francisco, dann ab durch die Mitte. Auf dem Interstate 80 fliegen wir über die Bay Bridge, schieben uns zwischen Berkeley und Oakland durch den dichten Stadtgürtel rund um die Bucht und landen nach einem großen Bogen um die Diablo Mountain Range im flachen Hinterland vor Stockton. Ein dichtes Netz von Kanälen und Flüssen füttert hier die Landwirtschafts-Industrie Kaliforniens, flaches Land, endlose Plantagen-Landschaften – wie ein krabbelndes Mechanik-Insekt durchquert das Auto diese Agrar-Wüste. Hinter Farmington wird die Fahrt auf dem Highway 4 nach Osten wieder spannend, die Plantagen-Endlosschleife löst sich in den ersten Hügeln auf, links und rechts zweigen schmale Sträßchen ab, die unter Eichen durch trockenes Gras streunen. Wie im Traum dahinsegeln, durch Telegraph City, dann bei Copperopolis nach Süden abbiegen und in Chinese Camp auf den Highway 49 wechseln. Ortsnamen wie Geschichtsstunden – besonders Europäer sind von dieser pragmatischen Art, Funktionsbezeichnungen auf ein Ortsschild zu bringen, regelrecht hingerissen. Vor dem inneren Auge wird dieses robuste Land ganz lebendig. Kupfer-Boom ab 1860, kleiner Bruder des Goldrauschs. Schwielige Hände entreißen den Hügeln das grünlich oxidierte Metall-Erz, dann beginnt ein langer Treck: Das Kupfer wird drüben in Stockton auf die Reise nach San Francisco geschickt, von dort geht es per Schiff – einmal um den ganzen Kontinent – an die Ostküste. Kupfer aus Kalifornien wird zu Gewehrkugeln im Großen Bürgerkrieg. Plötzlich wird dieser staubige Ort am Ende des Goldlands zum Knoten in einem großen Geschichten-Netz.

Du bist das Auto, Du bist Bewegung, Du bist die Straße. Anhalten beinahe unmöglich, ein Stopp würde sich jetzt wie Verrat anfühlen.
You are the car, you are movement, you are the road. Stopping would be all but impossible; it would feel like a betrayal.

pure curiosity. Your second option would be to visit the center of high-tech in Silicon Valley. However, the district is so industrial, sterile and boring that only die-hard Apple or Google fans sense the tingle of awestruck goose bumps at their respective headquarters in Cupertino and Mountain View. Check.

That leaves you with the third option – two days of high-voltage sightseeing in San Francisco, then head inland. We fly over the Bay Bridge on Interstate 80, squeezing ourselves between Berkeley and Oakland through the densely packed outskirts around the bay and, after making a big arc round the Diablo Mountains, end up in the flat hinterland near Stockton. A dense network of canals and rivers feeds California's agricultural industry. Flat land, endless plantations – the car crawls through this farmland desert like a mechanical insect. After Farmington, the journey east along Highway 4 becomes relaxing once more – the never-ending sea of plantations gives way to the first hills, narrow roads branching off left and right, wandering through dry grass in the shadow of oak trees. We glide in a dream world through Telegraph city, then turn south at Copperopolis, before joining Highway 49 in Chinese Camp. The place names are like history lessons – Europeans in particular are utterly smitten by this pragmatic and functional approach to road signage. Inside your mind, it brings this robust land to life. The copper boom began in 1860 as the little brother to the Gold Rush. Callused hands tore the greenish oxidized metal ore from the earth, before dispatching it on a lengthy voyage. From over in Stockton, the copper was sent to San Francisco, where it was loaded onto a ship and carried all the way around the continent to the east coast. Copper from California was

HIGHWAY 120

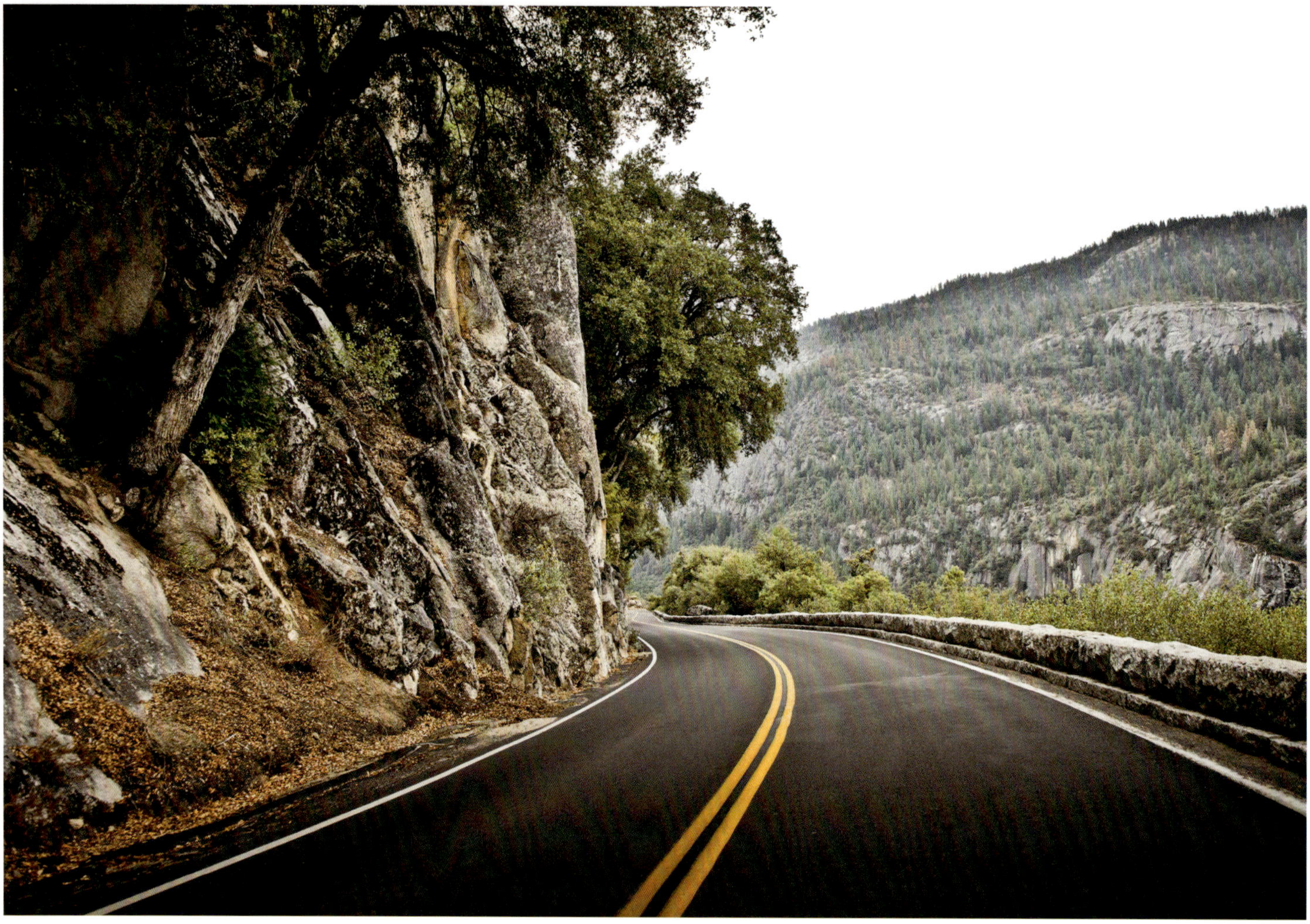

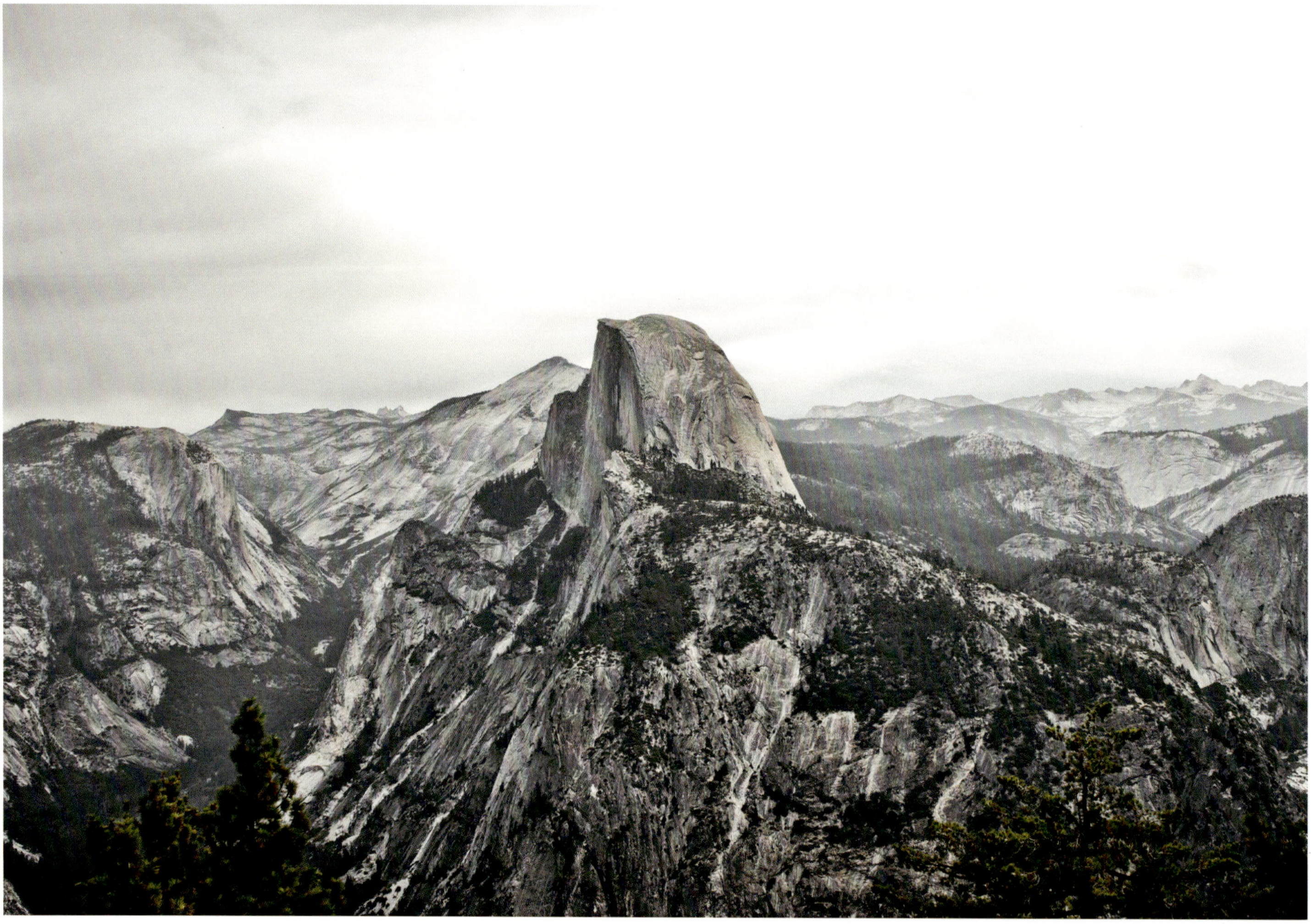

YOSEMITE

Chinese Camp? Klar, auch da tobt unter einer schläfrigen Schicht das wilde Leben einer abenteuerlichen Parallelwelt: Es sind chinesische Arbeiter, die Kalifornien von einer Wildnis in produktives Land verwandeln. Sie bauen die Eisenbahnen, sie rackern in den Minen – und die Weißen behandeln sie voller Verachtung. Also entstehen Dörfer und Städte für Chinesen. Chinese Camps. Nicht weit von hier sollen rivalisierende Chinesen-Gangs bei sogenannten Tong-Wars regelrechte Schlachten ausgefochten haben. Kaum zu glauben, wenn man in diesem trockenen, einsamen Land unterwegs ist. Aber hier erzählt jeder Baum Geschichten.

Bei Moccasin verlassen wir den Highway 49, rollen in Richtung Osten, das Auto schmiegt sich in den sanften Fluss dieser Straße hinauf in die Berge. Sanfte Radien und weiche Kuppen, Asphalt, der stetig zwischen rau und seidenweich wechselt. Innerhalb von wenigen Meilen bleibt das staubhustende Tal des Goldlands zurück, die Eichen verschwinden und duftende Nadelbäume schließen sich immer dichter zusammen. Dies ist der Einstieg in die Sierra Nevada Mountains. Vor gut zehn Millionen Jahren hätte man hier den Aufstieg eines monumentalen Granitblocks aus 10 Kilometern Erdkrusten-Tiefe beobachten können, der die Erdoberfläche dann in Richtung Westen abkippen ließ. Auf diesem Rücken reiten wir jetzt in Richtung Natur-Spektakel; die zunehmende Anzahl von Wohnmobilen auf großer „Alle-Sehenswürdigkeiten-Amerikas-abklappern-bevor-es-nicht-mehr-geht"-Tour ist in diesem Teil der Welt immer ein erstes Signal für kommende Wunder.

Irgendwann windet sich die Straße andächtig unter gigantischen Riesenmammutbäumen hindurch. Cabriofahrer dürfen spätestens jetzt das Verdeck nach hinten werfen, denn ab hier spielt sich alles Wesentliche in der Vertikalen ab: Plötzlich ragen um einen flachen, weiten Talboden riesenhafte Granitwände auf, der massige Block des „El Capitan", und ganz am Ende des Tals die völlig glatt abstürzende Nordwest-Wand des „Half Dome". Stehenbleiben. Kopf in den Nacken. Und kein Wort sagen.

turned into ammunition during the American Civil War. Suddenly this dusty place at the end of gold country became the hub of a huge historical network. Chinese Camp? There, too, the wild existence of an adventurous parallel world ran riot beneath a sleepy outer layer. It was Chinese workers who transformed California from a wilderness to a productive land. They built railroads, they toiled in the mines – and the white people treated them with contempt. Villages and towns popped up to house the Chinese – Chinese Camps. Not far from here, Chinese gangs allegedly fought pitched battles in the so-called Tong Wars. It's hard to believe as you travel through this arid, desolate land. But here, every tree has a story to tell.

We leave Highway 49 at Moccasin heading east, the car melding with the gentle flow of the road up into the mountains. We roll through soft radii and over gentle crests on asphalt that keeps switching back and forth between rough and silky smooth. A few miles later, we've left the dust-strewn valley of gold country behind; the oak trees disappear and scented pine trees draw ever closer together. This is the climb into the Sierra Nevada Mountains. More than ten million years ago, you would have been able to watch as a monumental block of granite rose up from ten kilometers beneath the earth's crust, making the surface of the earth tip over toward the west. We're now riding along this ridge toward a spectacle of nature. In this part of the world, the increasing number of motor homes on "let's see all the sights of America while we still can" tours is always a first sign of the wonder that lies ahead. At some point, the road begins to wind its way reverently beneath the towering mantle of giant redwood trees. By now, convertible drivers should definitely put the top down, because all that matters from here on in is vertical. Suddenly, there are colossal granite walls soaring skyward all around the broad, flat valley floor – the massive block of "El Capitan" and, right at the end of the valley, the completely smooth, sheer face of the northwest wall of the "Half Dome". Stand still, lean your head as far back as it will go and say absolutely nothing.

YOSEMITE

SAN FRANCISCO YOSEMITE

San Francisco gehört zu den wohl schönsten und spannendsten Städten der Welt. Auch hier hat eine Stadtrundfahrt mit dem Auto ganz besonderen Reiz – Steve McQueen-Fans dürfte die Berg- und Talfahrt über San Franciscos steile Hügelstraßen natürlich ganz besonders anziehen. Danach verlassen wir die Pazifikküste in Richtung Osten, die Reise geht nun ins historische Kalifornien des Goldrauschs. Vom milden Klima der Küste über die fruchtbaren Ebenen im Hinterland bis ins trockene Land am Fuß der Sierra Nevada durchqueren wir auf dieser Fahrt eine Vielzahl von Klima- und Vegetationszonen, am Ende der Fahrt steht der Aufstieg ins Yosemite Valley. Dieser hochgelegene Nationalpark zieht jedes Jahr über drei Millionen Besucher an; beim Blick in das wilde Tal, umgeben von schroffen Bergriesen, ist schnell klar, weshalb Yosemite zu den Landschafts-Ikonen der gesamten USA gehört.

—

San Francisco is one of the world's most captivating and thrilling cities. Here, too, a city tour by car has a very particular appeal – Steve McQueen fans are, of course, especially drawn to the ups and downs of San Francisco's steep hill streets. We then leave the Pacific Coast heading eastward. Our journey is now taking us into the historical California of the Gold Rush era. From the mild coastal climate, through the fertile hinterland to the arid prairieland at the foot of the Sierra Nevada, this drive takes us through a wide spectrum of climate and vegetation zones, with the trip culminating in the ascent into Yosemite Valley. This high-altitude national park draws more than three million visitors every year. Just one glance into the wild valley surrounded by rugged mountains is all it takes to see exactly why Yosemite is one of the most iconic landscapes in the whole of the USA.

310 KM • 4 STUNDEN // 192 MILES • 4 HOURS

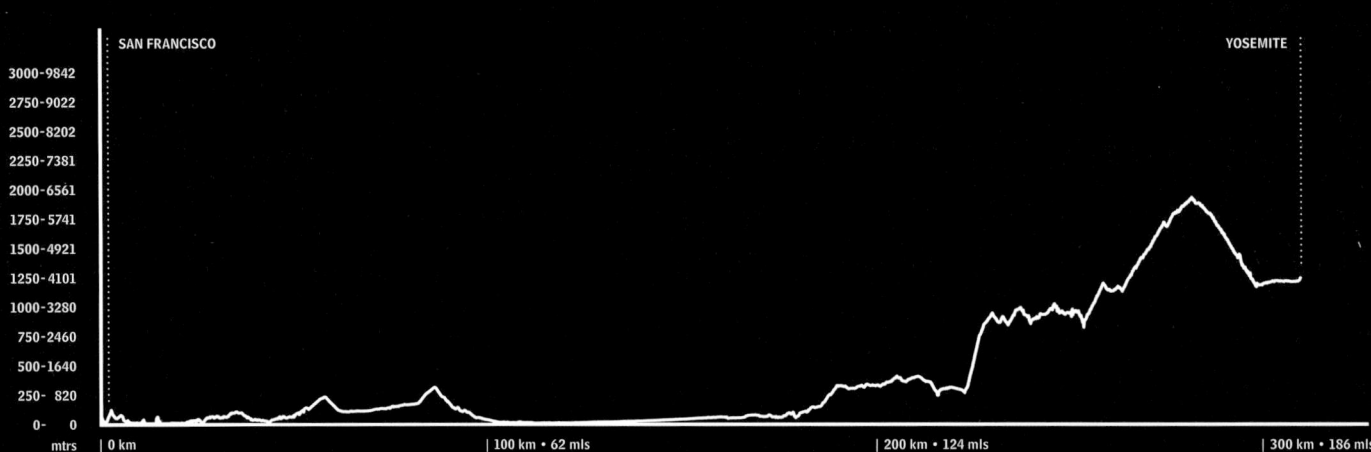

USA • KALIFORNIEN

YOSEMITE
LAS VEGAS

815 KM • 8 STUNDEN // 506 MILES • 8 HOURS

Yosemite Valley. Orte wie dieser besitzen eine magische Gravitation, ihre atemberaubende Erhabenheit und beklemmende Schönheit lösen den sehnsüchtigen Wunsch aus, vom distanzierten Beobachter zum Teil des Ganzen zu werden.

—

Yosemite Valley. Places like this possess a magical gravitational pull; their breathtaking grandeur and oppressive beauty inspire a yearning within those observing from a distance to become part of the whole.

HOTELS

MANDALAY BAY
3950 S LAS VEGAS BLVD
LAS VEGAS, NV 89119
WWW.MANDALAYBAY.COM

FURNANCE CREEK INN
328 GREENLAND BLVD.
DEATH VALLEY
TEL. +1 760 786 2345
WWW.FURNACECREEKRESORT.COM

Wer an den Surfspots der Pazifikküste paralysiert aufs Wasser hinausstarrt und sich nichts mehr wünscht, als im nächsten Moment auf einem schmalen Surfboard von Acht-Meter-Brechern zum Grund des Ozeans gerammt zu werden oder eine dunkelgrüne Röhre aus Tonnen von schäumendem Wasser zu reiten, der wird auch von den Felstürmen des Tals in der Sierra Nevada magisch angezogen sein. Im Gras sitzen und mit den Augen durch Spalten und Grate steigen, den rauen Granit unter den Fingern spüren, die Wärme des Gesteins. Menschen sind so: Wer unten ist, will hinauf. Man müsste, man könnte doch ... Was es wohl dort oben zu sehen gibt? Und dann ist dieses Tal ja auch durch seine Konzentration so eigentümlich, der Kessel aus 1000-Meter-Wänden und die explodierende Vegetation am Talboden erzeugen das faszinierende Gefühl eines eigenen Universums. Als gäbe es hinter den Bergen nichts Relevantes mehr. Tausende Besucher werden jedes Jahr ins enge Yosemite Valley gespült und nur wenige stellen sich daher der herzzerreißenden Dramatik des ganzen National Parks.

Unser Elfer weiß es besser. Leise knurrend nehmen wir die Nordausfahrt zurück, dann die CA-120 über den 3031 Meter hohen Tioga Pass im Nordosten. Hier ist die Ost-Abbruchkante des Gebirges erreicht. Hinter dem Pass stürzt die Straße durch eine albtraumartige Schutt-Landschaft innerhalb weniger Meilen steil hinunter. Wenn der Pazifik Regenwolken füttert, laden die ihr Wasser im Westen des Gebirges ab. Dort drüben ist das Land fett und grün, hier im Osten sagt die Wüste Hallo: trocken, karg, Mars und Mond – der Weg zum Mono Lake ist ein Schlag ins Gesicht für Harmoniesüchtige. Und am See angekommen wird nichts besser. Immer noch beinahe 2000 Meter hoch gelegen, pfeift hier ein beißender Wind über das Tal-Becken, der runde See mit seinen

Anyone who stands at the surfing beaches along the Pacific coast and stares transfixed out at the water, wishing nothing more than to be rammed at any moment from a narrow surfboard onto the ocean floor by 8-meter breakers, or to ride through a dark green tunnel of churning surf will also be magically drawn to the rock stacks in the valleys of the Sierra Nevada. Sit in the grass and imagine yourself climbing through cracks and crevices, feel the rough granite beneath your fingers, the warmth of the stone. That's how people are: If you're at the bottom of something, you want to reach the top. You have to. Of course you can do it ... What must it be like up there? And, of course, this valley is so utterly unique, partly because of its concentration: This enormous cauldron with 1000-meter walls and the explosion of vegetation on the valley floor creates an amazing feeling of being a universe all of its own, as if there was nothing of any relevance behind the mountains. Thousands of visitors spill into the narrow Yosemite Valley every year, and only a few of them surrender themselves to the heartrending drama of the whole national park.

Our Carrera knows better. Snarling quietly, we take the northbound exit back, then the CA-120 over the 3031-meter Tioga Pass in the northeast, reaching the eastern rim of the mountain range. On the other side of the pass, the road falls steeply away in the space of a just few miles through a nightmarish boulder landscape. When the Pacific feeds rain clouds, they offload their water in the west of the mountain range. Over there, the land is lush and green. Here in the east, we're faced with desert – parched and sparse, a Mars and Moonscape. The way to Mono Lake is a slap in the face for anyone seeking harmony. And things don't improve any when you reach the lake itself. At an altitude of almost 2000 meters, a biting

TIOGA PASS

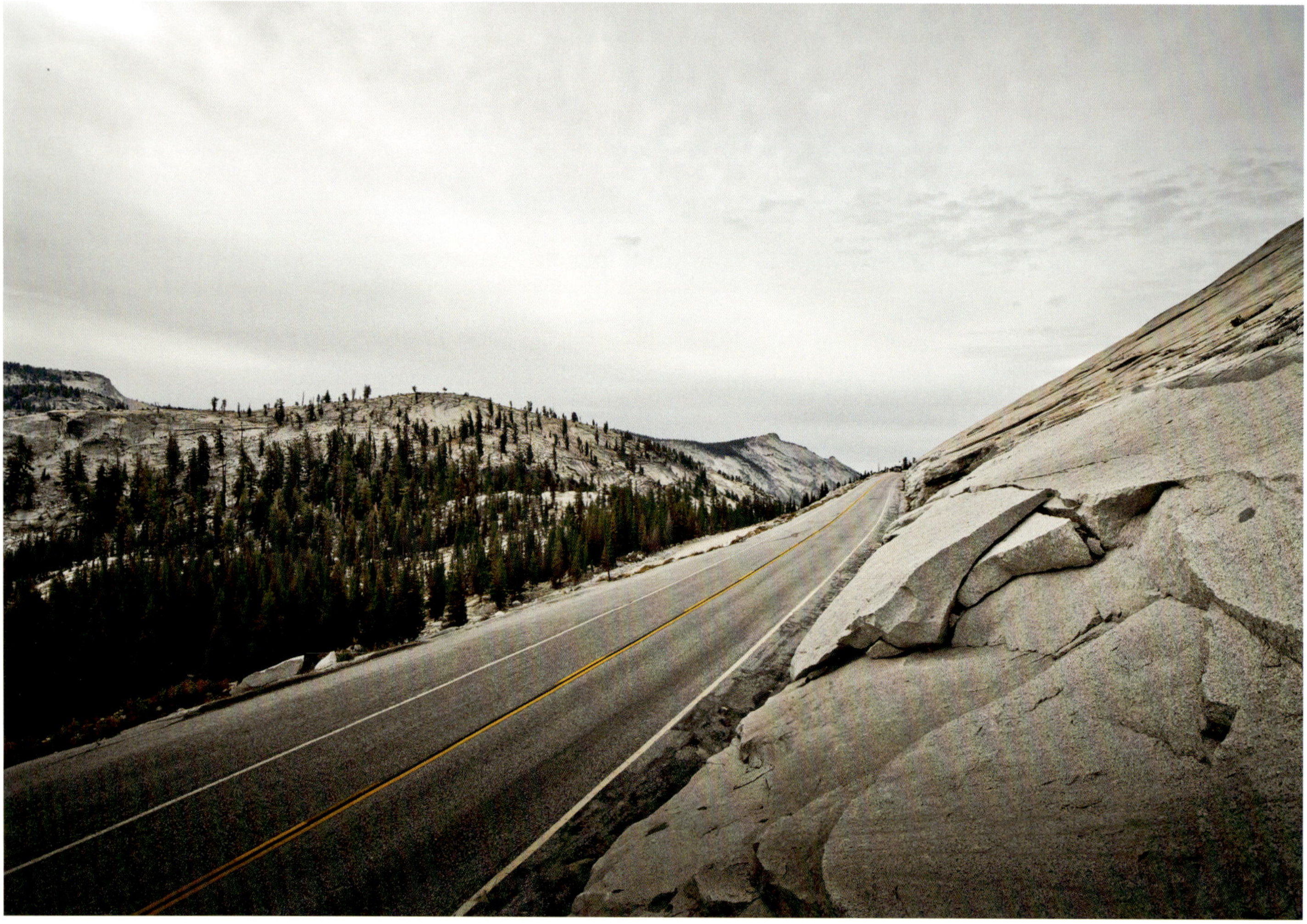

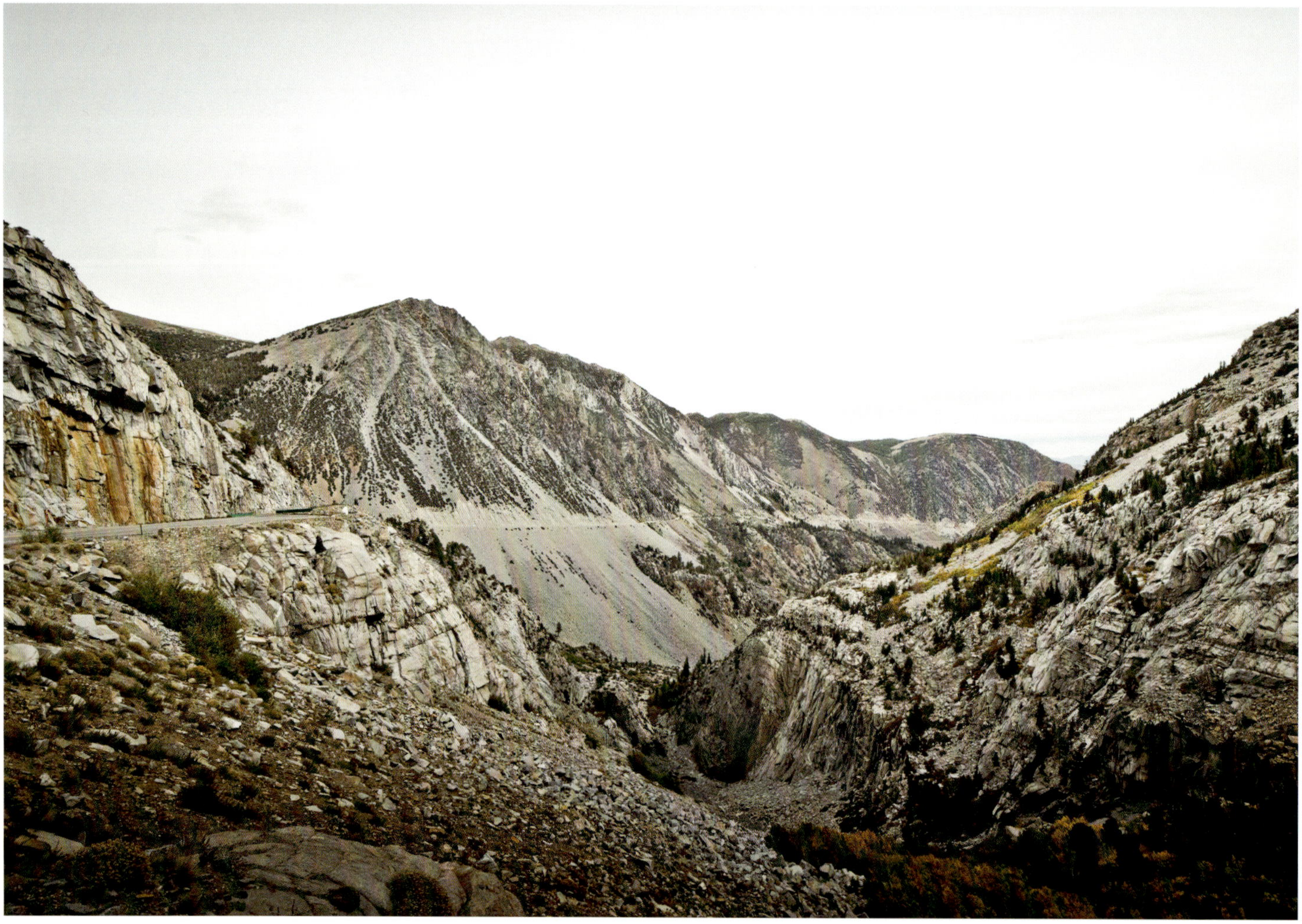

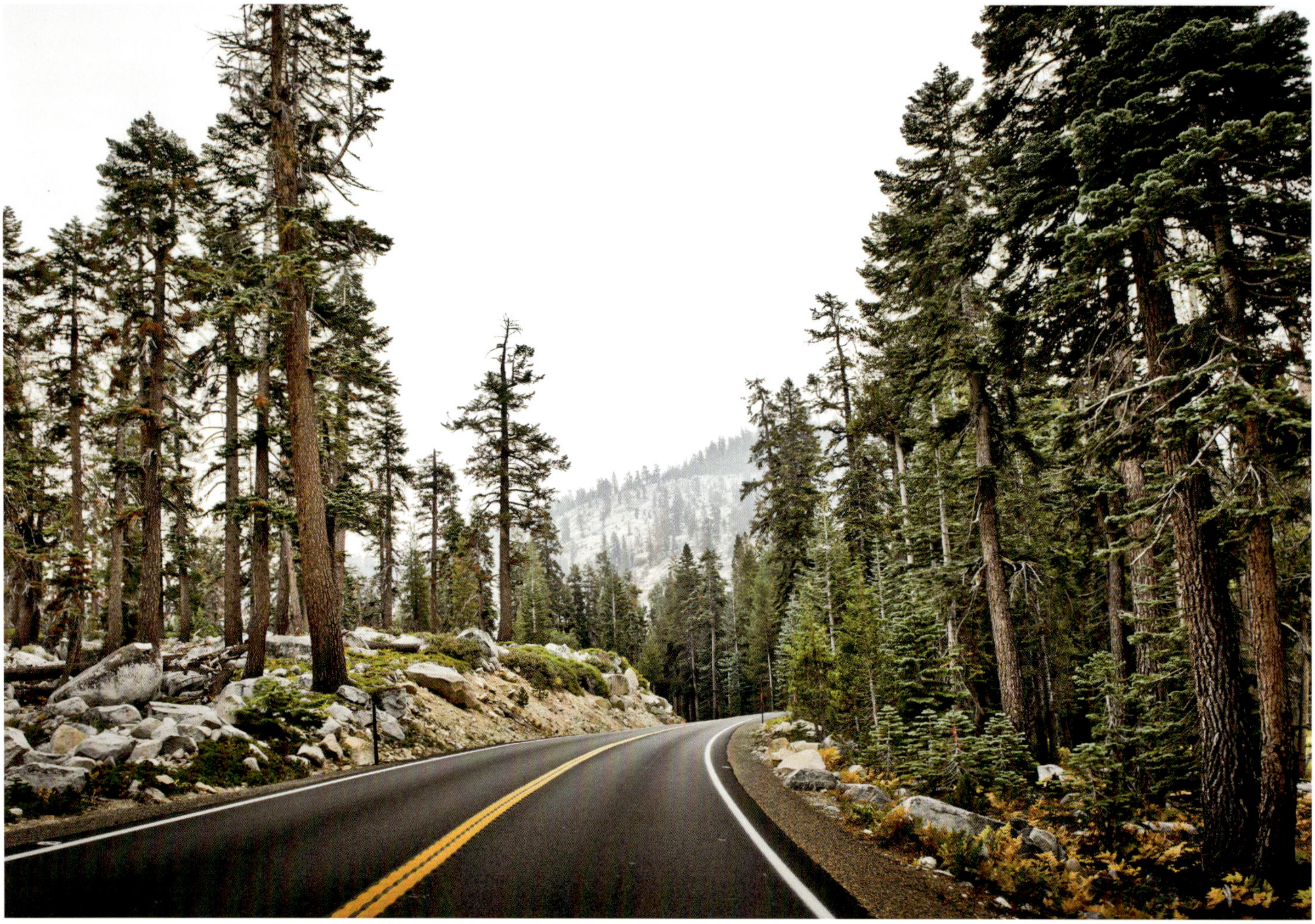

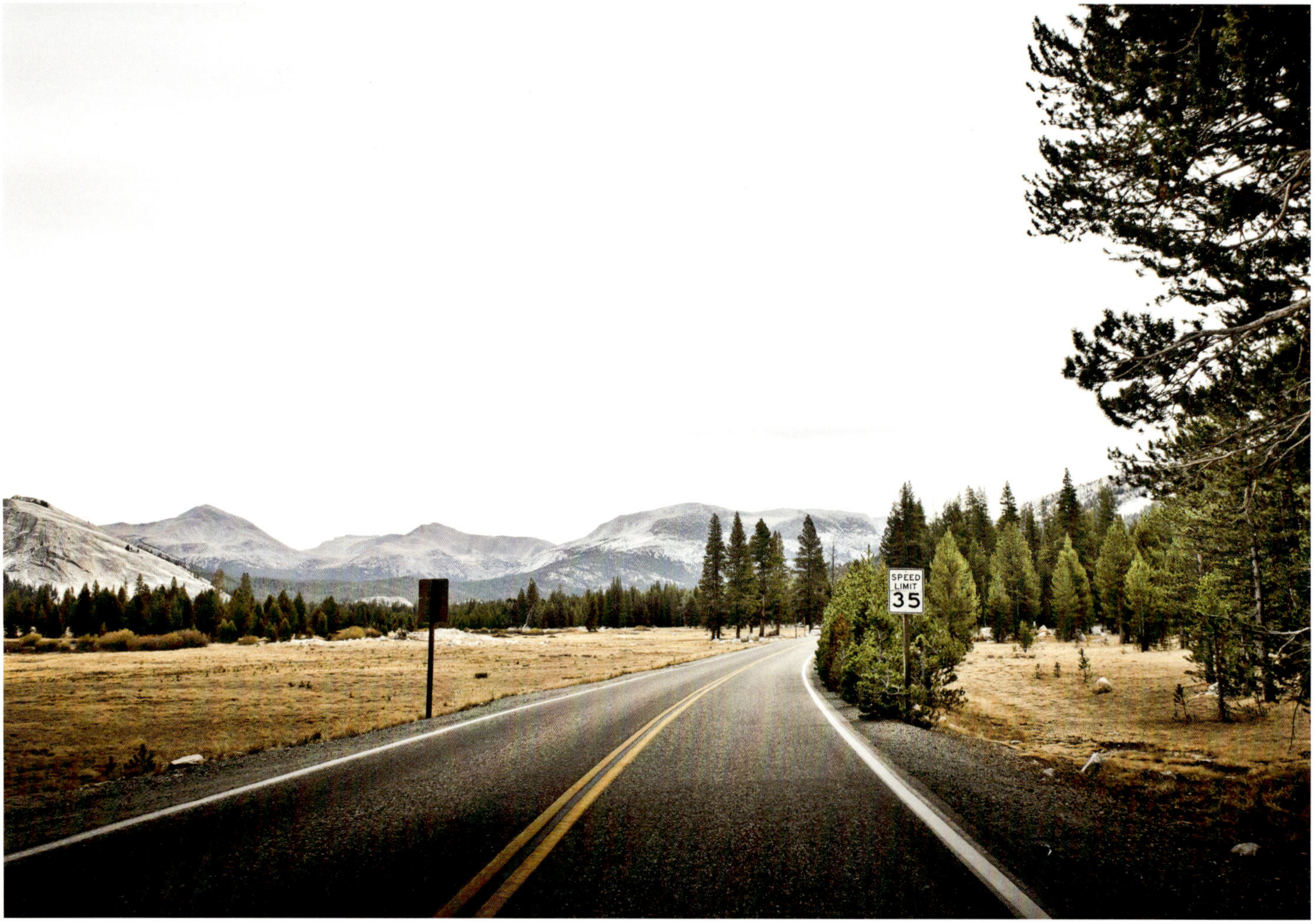
SPEED LIMIT
35

> Die atmosphärische Umstellung auf die nächsten 300 Meilen ist nun innerhalb weniger Minuten erfolgt, emotionale Schockfrostung sozusagen.
>
> Acclimatization for the next 300 miles is dealt with in the space of just a few minutes – a kind of emotional shock freezing, if you will.

Vulkan-Inseln ist mit salzigem Natron-Wasser gefüllt. Die Welt ist hier uralt und wenn ein abflussloser See unter diesen Bedingungen ein paar Millionen Jahre Zeit hat, verwandelt er sich eben in eine spannende Mischung aus H2O, Salzen, Schwefel, Bor und Arsen. Oder mit anderen Worten ausgedrückt: Einen Badestrand suchen Sie am Mono Lake vergebens. Angeln ist hier zwar erlaubt, aber erfolglos – bestimmende Lebensformen sind Mini-Salzkrebse und Salzfliegen.

Etwas Gutes hat das Apokalypse-Szenario unterhalb der schneebedeckten Sierra Nevada-Gipfel aber doch: Die atmosphärische Umstellung auf die nächsten 300 Meilen ist nun innerhalb weniger Minuten erfolgt, emotionale Schockfrostung sozusagen. In Richtung Benton und Bishop wird das Dauer-Mantra der Straße – Steine, Gestrüpp, Steine, Gestrüpp – nur selten unterbrochen, man fährt zum ersten Mal auf dieser Kalifornien-Reise durch ein Land, das alle Gedanken verstummen lässt. Grauenvolle Menschenfeindlichkeit, beängstigend monoton, Geologie und Biologie im frühen Skizzenstadium. Wer wissen will, wie unser Planet eigentlich gedacht ist, ohne die dünne Schicht aus Vegetation, Fauna und menschlicher Zivilisation, sollte hierher kommen. Erstaunlicherweise setzt beim Blick ins schroffe, uralte Gesicht unserer Mutter Erde plötzlich eine verblüffende Sorglosigkeit ein: Mobiltelefone funktionieren hier draußen nur selten, der Informationsfluss versiegt, Moden und Trends, Technologie und Zeitgeist, Weltpolitik und selbst die kleinen, individuellen Sorgen werden hier draußen sonderbar blass. Drei Tage in der Wüste, und Dir ist vollkommen egal, ob Google nun gerade China gekauft

wind whistles along the valley floor. The round lake with its volcanic islands is filled with saline soda water. This is a primeval world here, and when a lake with no outlet spends a couple of million years under these conditions, it turns into a fascinating mixture of H2O, salts, sulfur, boron and arsenic. Or in other words – don't waste your time looking for a bathing beach at Mono Lake. Fishing is permitted, but pointless – the predominant lifeforms are tiny brine shrimp and alkali flies.

But there is something positive to be gained from the apocalyptic scene beneath the snow-covered Sierra Nevada summit: Acclimatization for the next 300 miles is dealt with in the space of just a few minutes – a kind of emotional shock freezing, if you will. Heading for Benton and Bishop, the road's incessant mantra – rocks, scrub, rocks, scrub – is rarely interrupted. For the first time on this California trip, you travel through a land that numbs all thought. This is harrowing hostility, frightening monotony, geology and biology at the early sketch stage. If you want to know what the original blueprint for our planet looks like, without its thin layer of vegetation, fauna and human civilization, this is where you need to come. Amazingly, with this view of the abrasive, primeval face of our mother Earth comes a sudden and perplexing sense of release. Cell phones rarely work out here, the flow of information runs dry. Fashions and trends, technology and zeitgeist, global politics and even small, individual worries pale into insignificance out here. Three days in the desert and you really don't care whether or not Google has just bought China or if

MONO LAKE

hat oder lila Locken die neueste Männermode sind. Die Wüste twittert nicht. Du atmest ein, Du atmest aus. Genau jetzt. Nicht mehr und nicht weniger.

Spätestens jetzt ist für alle Europäer die Stunde der Wahrheit gekommen, denn das schnurgerade Asphaltband in der Ewigkeit besitzt eine bedrohliche, bewusstseinsverschiebende Dynamik. Alles, was Du je über Geraden oder Zeitreisen gehört hast, wird hier entsetzliche Wahrheit. Je weiter unser Auto ins Owens Valley vorstößt, desto lockerer sitzt die Psyche. Und dabei haben wir den bösartigsten Streckenteil noch vor uns. Bis Lone Pine fällt achtsamen Synapsen irgendwo im Halb-Bewusstsein lediglich auf, dass der einsame Fahrer andere Vertreter der Spezies Homo sapiens oder Anzeichen ihrer Anwesenheit mit eigenartigem Staunen wahrzunehmen beginnt. Gibt es noch mehr von meiner Sorte? Was tun Menschen hier? Dann hilft der Sprung aus dem Owens Valley über die Panamint-Berge mit ihren kurvigen Passagen, um für einige Zeit auf andere Gedanken zu kommen. Auch die folgende Pinto Peak-Bergkette sorgt ein letztes Mal für etwas Ablenkung. Beim dann folgenden Blick ins unter einem eisblauen Himmel glühende Death Valley ahnen allerdings auch eher ungerührte Naturen, dass die Strecke bis hierher höchstens als Generalprobe gelten kann. Fast schuldbewusst führt die Straße hinunter ins Tal, rollt schüchtern zwischen Geröll und Vulkan-Schutt hin und her, bis sie am Talboden angelangt ist. Beinahe etwas unwillig löst man sich dann von den Bergen, dieser letzten Kontur und letzten Definierbarkeit, bevor man tapfer in das schier endlose Tal hinausfährt. Den Blick immer auf die dunstige Bergkette am anderen Horizont geheftet. Mit aller Vorsicht und sämtlichen guten

purple curls are the latest fashion for men. The desert doesn't tweet. You breathe in, you breathe out – here and now. No more and no less.

By now at the very latest, the moment of truth has dawned on all Europeans, because the dead-straight strip of blacktop disappearing into eternity possesses a threatening, consciousness-altering dynamic. All you've ever heard about straights or time travel becomes an appalling truth here. The farther our car advances into Owens Valley, the more the psyche is shaken. And the worst is yet to come. By Lone Pine, attentive synapses notice somewhere in the sub-consciousness that the solitary driver begins to perceive other members of the homo sapiens species or signs of their presence with a strange astonishment. Are there more like me? What are people doing here? Then the leap out of Owens Valley over the winding passes of the Panamint Mountains diverts your attention to other thoughts for a while. The Pinto Peak chain also offers some distraction for one last time. After that, one look into the searing Death Valley beneath an ice-blue sky causes even unflappable types to think that maybe the route so far has been nothing more than a dress rehearsal. The road leads almost guiltily into the valley, wandering sheepishly to and fro between boulders and volcanic rock until it reaches the valley floor. It's almost with a degree of reluctance that you let go of the mountains – these last contours and final elements of definition, before you venture valiantly into this never-ending valley. You keep your eyes glued firmly to the hazy mountain range on the other horizon. You're fully equipped with every possibly caution and all manner of good advice, the trunk and even the glove

Man kann im Death Valley verdursten oder erfrieren – aber auch von der Highway Control aus dem Helikopter abgeschossen werden.

You can die of thirst or the cold in Death Valley, but you can also be shot with the camera of a helicopter by Highway Control.

Ratschlägen ausgestattet, Kofferraum und selbst Handschuhfach mit rationalen Warnungen und Schauermärchen gut gefüllt. Der Tank ist voll, ein Dutzend Wasserflaschen gluckern beruhigend vor sich hin. Eine kleine Gruppe von Shoshone-Indianern ist im Valley zuhause – alle anderen Menschen sollten sich besser nicht mit dieser Landschaft anlegen. Haftung ist hier ausgeschlossen, das Death Valley lässt sich nicht verklagen. Also immer schön demütig bleiben, keinen Unfug machen und trotzdem das Tempolimit einhalten. Man kann im Death Valley verdursten oder erfrieren – aber auch von der Highway Control aus dem Helikopter abgeschossen werden. Geschwindigkeit wird nach dem ersten Lichtjahr sowieso relativ: In wahnwitzigem Tempo strebt man hinaus ins Tal, immer dem anderen Ufer entgegen, und irgendwann stellt man fest, dass da überhaupt nichts näher kommt. Nur die Berge im Rückspiegel werden zuerst klein, dann werden auch sie zum gegen die Himmelskuppel gepinselten Bühnenbild. Dein Auto und Du in einer XXL-Truman Show.

Jetzt nur nicht die Nerven verlieren, irgendwann wirken die Berge voraus tatsächlich ein wenig größer. Zeit, nach rechts abzubiegen. Beatty Junction, Furnace Creek, Zabriskie Point, ein Abstecher hoch zur Dantes View Road – der Blick ins Tal ist „amazing" – und rüber nach Death Valley Junction, dann haben wir Kalifornien einmal durchquert: vom Pazifik bis an die Grenze im Osten. Weil die Grenze nach Nevada aber kaum wahrnehmbar ist, fahren wir einfach weiter. Rollen durch Pahrump, hüpfen über die Spring Mountains – und dann ist da plötzlich im monochromen Braun der Wüste eine optische Störung. Da vorne sind Häuser. Viele Häuser. Große Häuser. Die Abendsonne wird zum orangeroten Spotlight. Die Show geht los. Hello, Baby! Hello, Las Vegas!

box well packed with rational warnings and horror stories. The tank is full and a dozen bottles of water gurgle comfortingly away to themselves. The valley is home to a small group of Shoshone Indians – all others would be best advised to steer clear of this landscape. There's no accountability. Death Valley cannot be sued. So remain humble, don't cause trouble and obey the speed limit – while you can die of thirst or the cold in Death Valley, but you can also be shot with the camera of a helicopter by Highway Control. But after the first light year, speed becomes relative anyway. You forge into the valley at an insane pace, constantly aiming for the other side, but eventually you realize that absolutely nothing is getting any closer. To begin with, only the mountains in the rear-view mirror are getting smaller, until they too become a painted backdrop against the massive expanse of sky. It's you and your car in an XXL Truman Show.

Don't lose your nerve now. At some point, the mountains ahead really do start to look a tiny bit bigger. It's time to turn right. Beatty Junction, Furnace Creek, Zabriskie Point, Dantes View Road with its amazing lookout, over to Death Valley Junction and, finally, we reach the other side of California – from the Pacific to the eastern border. Because the border to Nevada is barely noticeable, we simply keep on going. We roll through Pahrump, hop over Spring Mountains – and then suddenly an optical illusion shimmers in the monochrome brown of the desert. There are houses in front of us; lots of houses; big houses. The evening sun turns into an orange-red spotlight. The show is about to start. Hello, Baby! Hello, Las Vegas!

AT LONE PINE

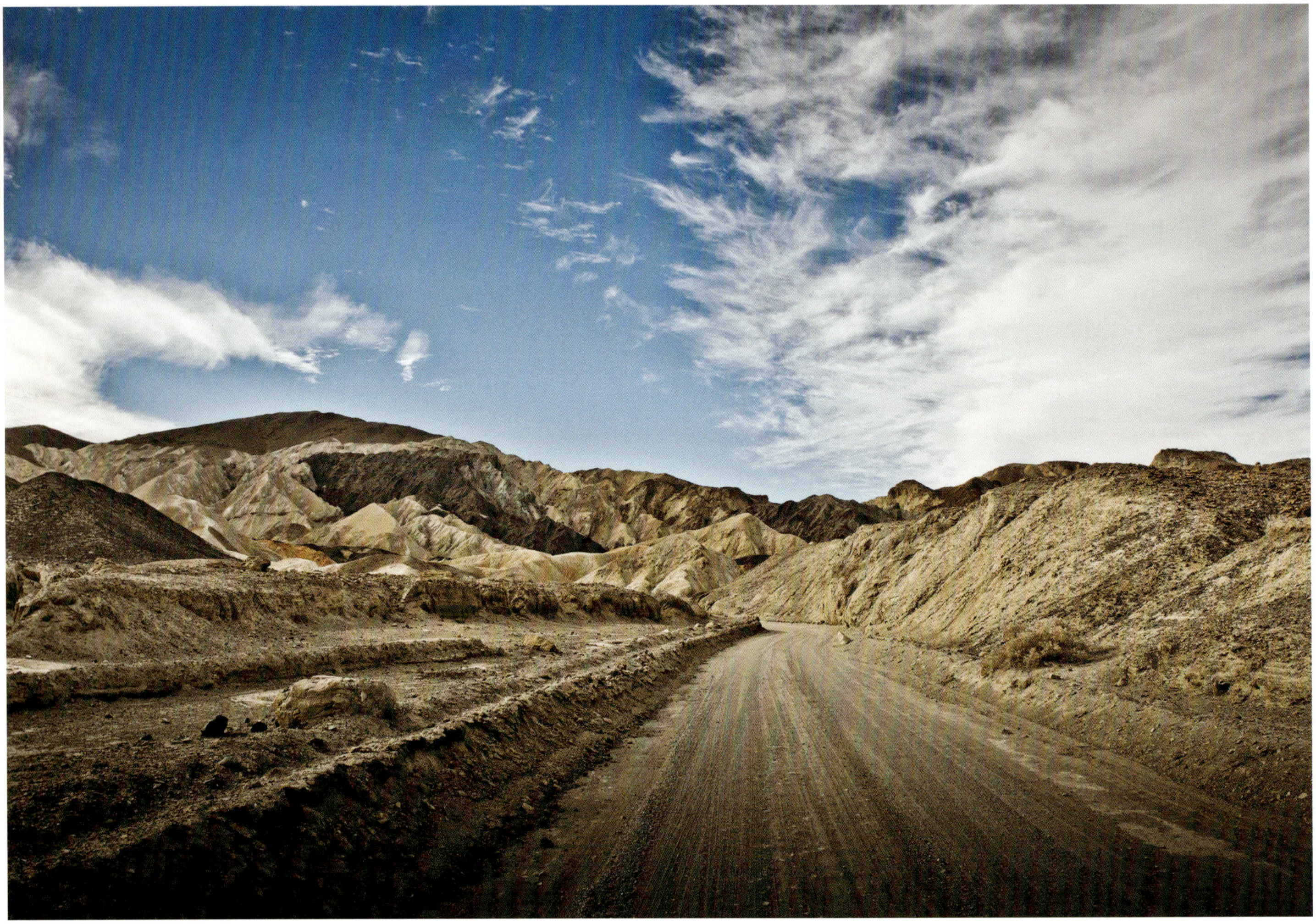

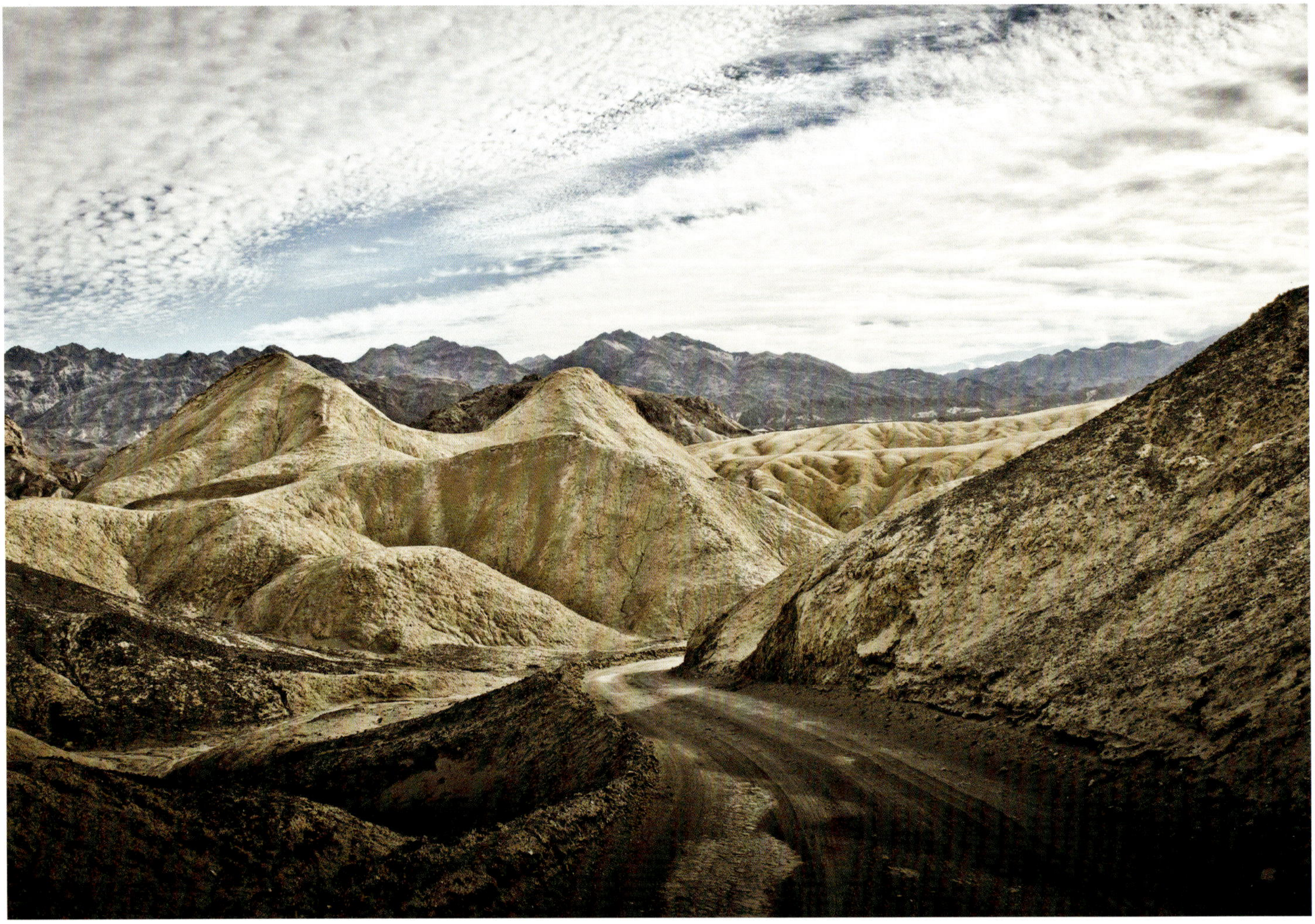

DEATH VALLEY

DEATH VALLEY

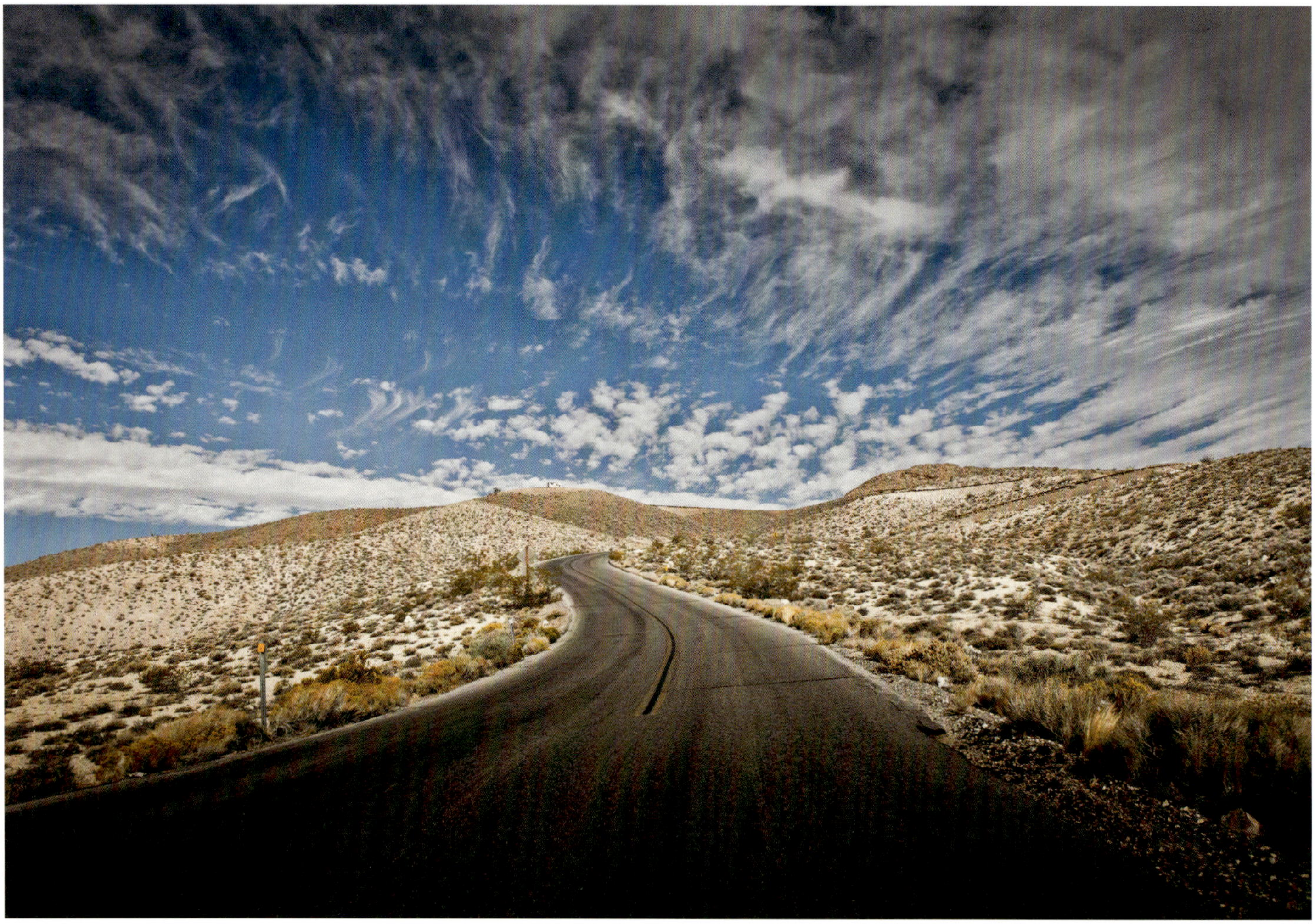

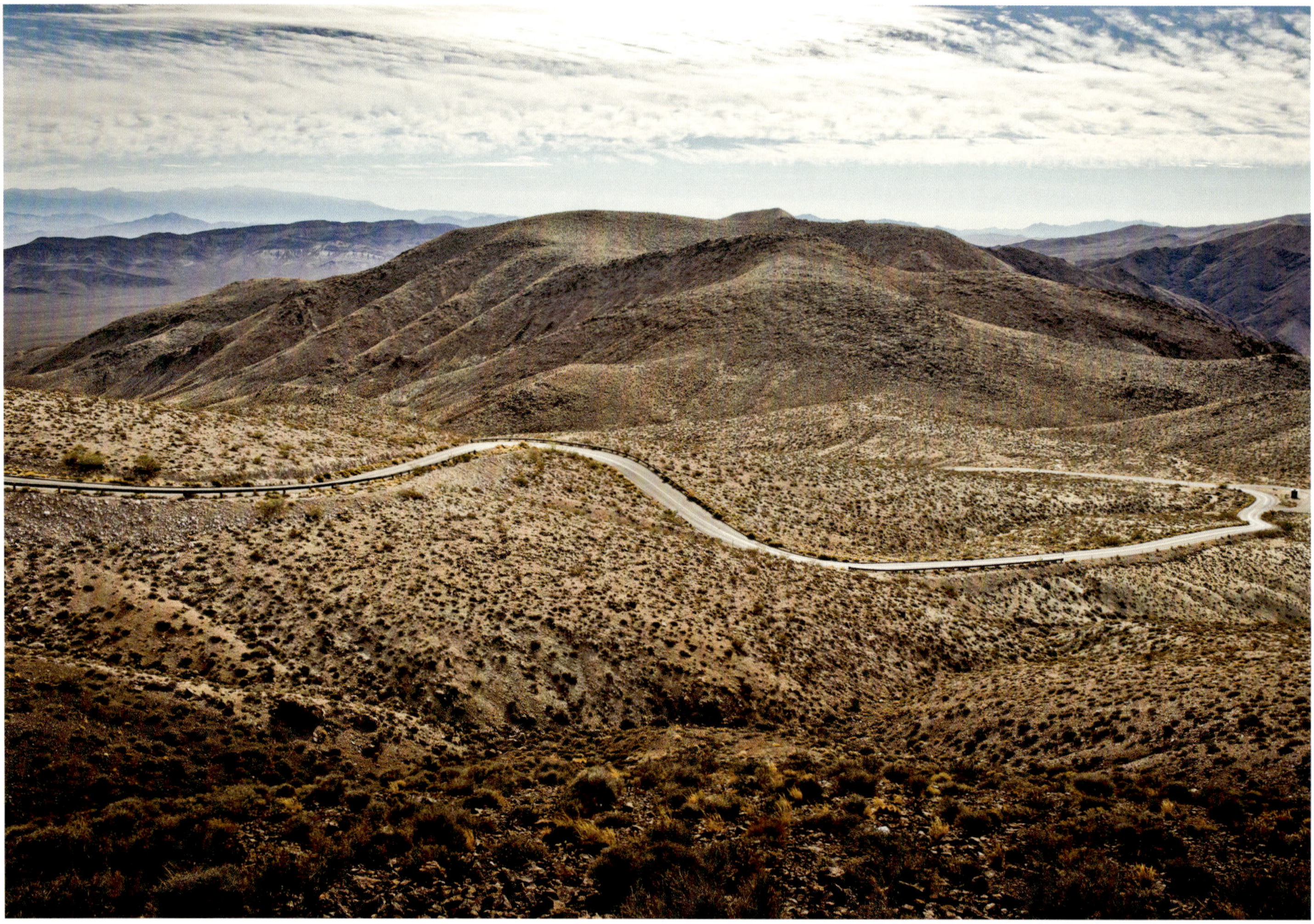

DANTES VIEW

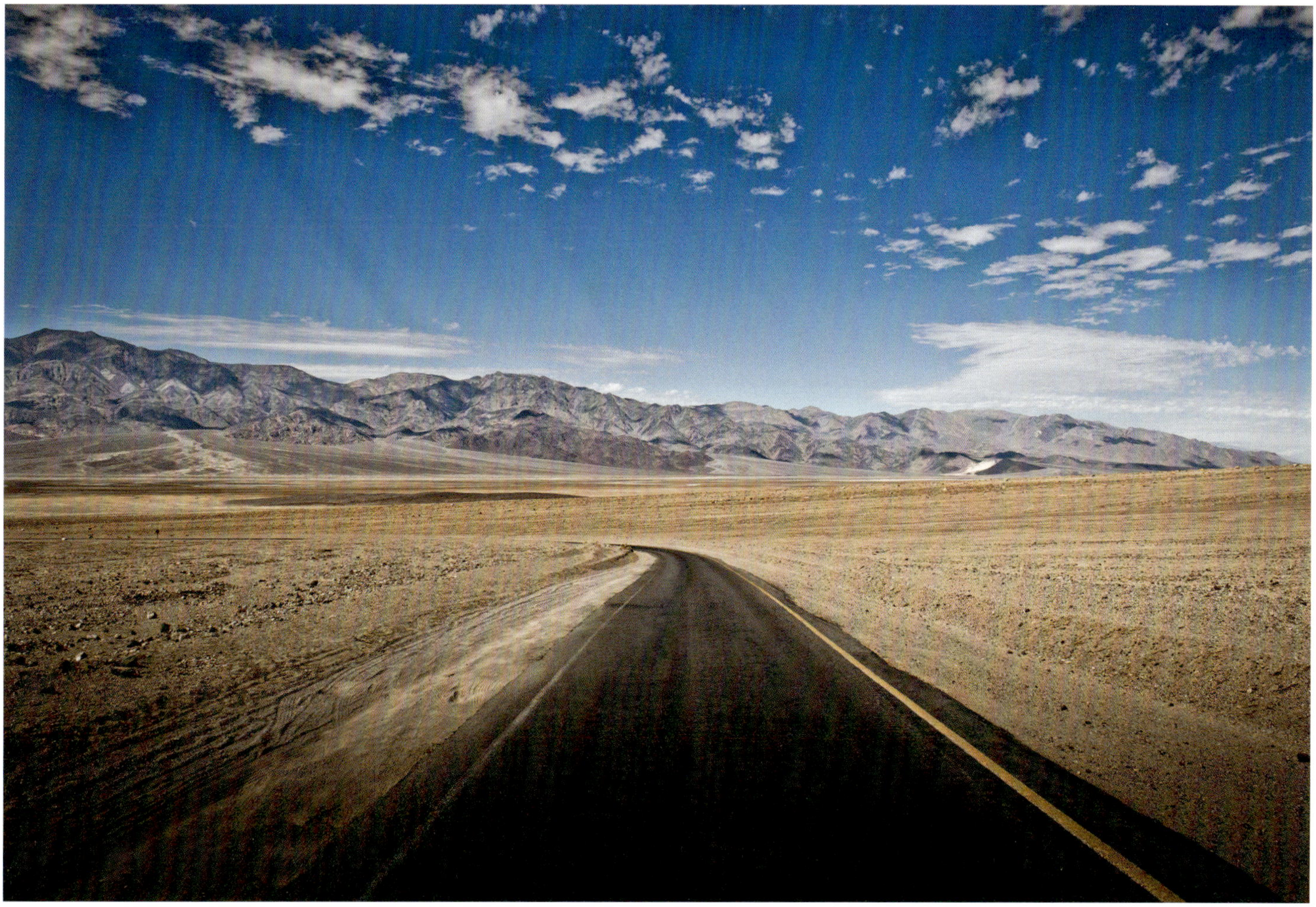
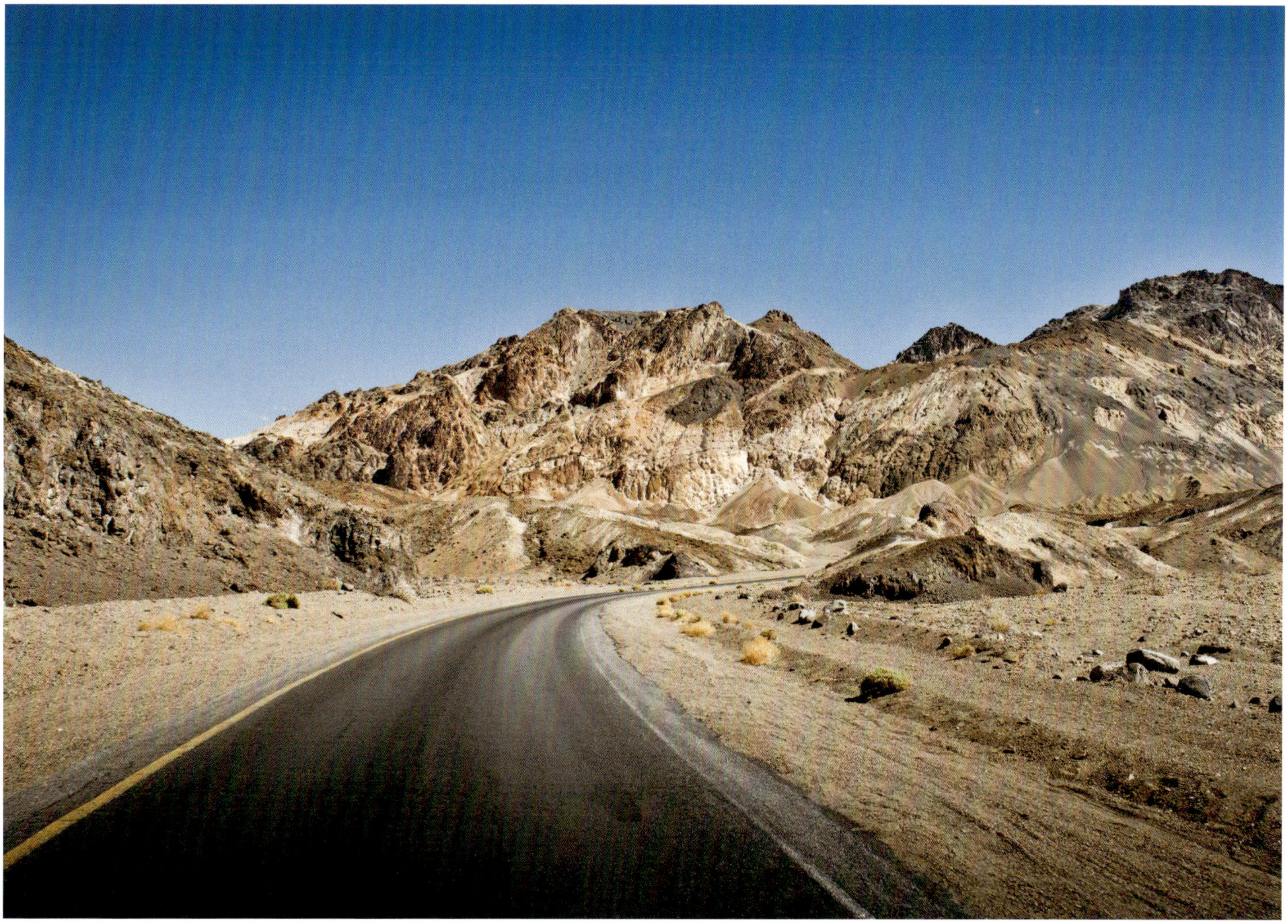

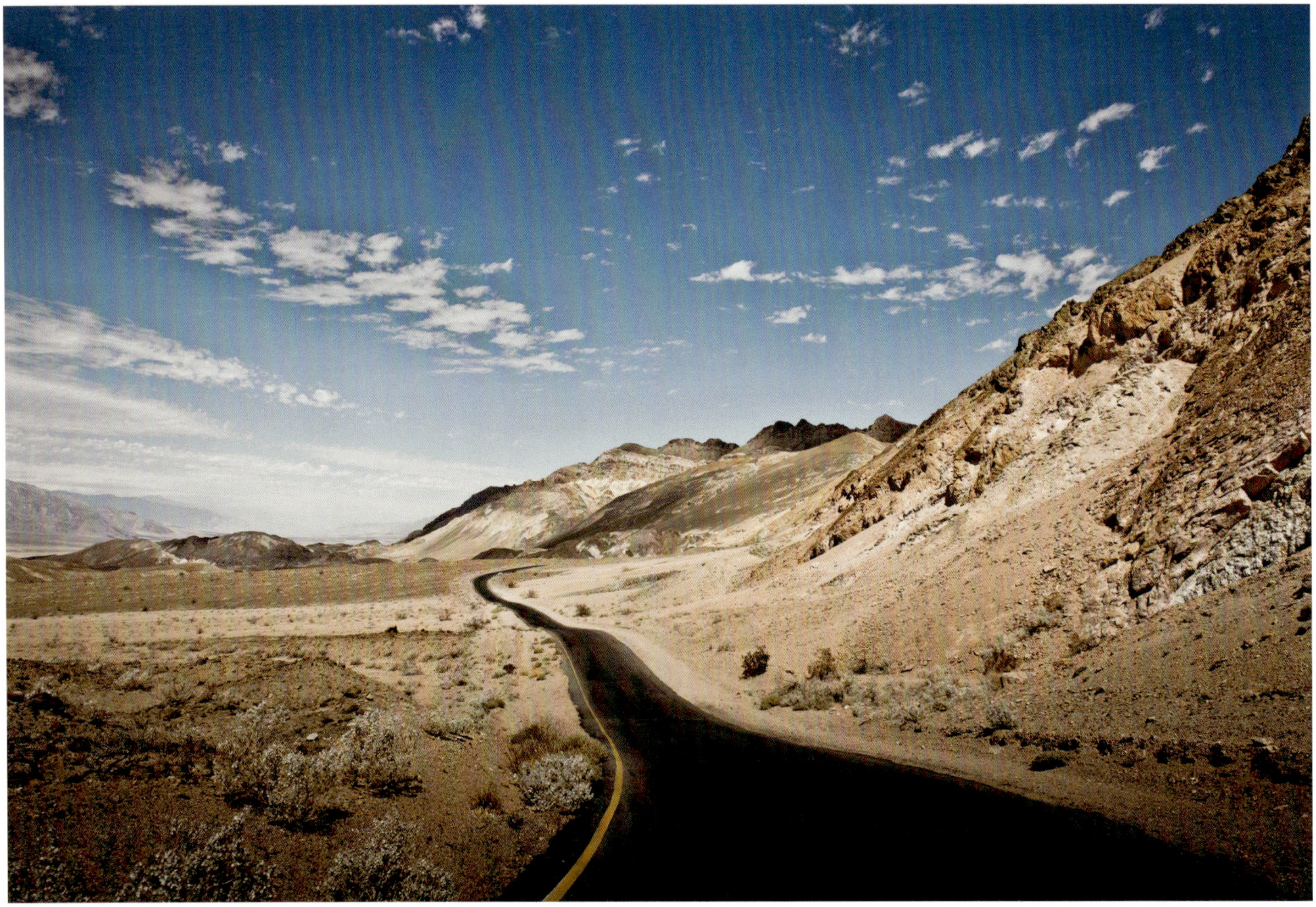

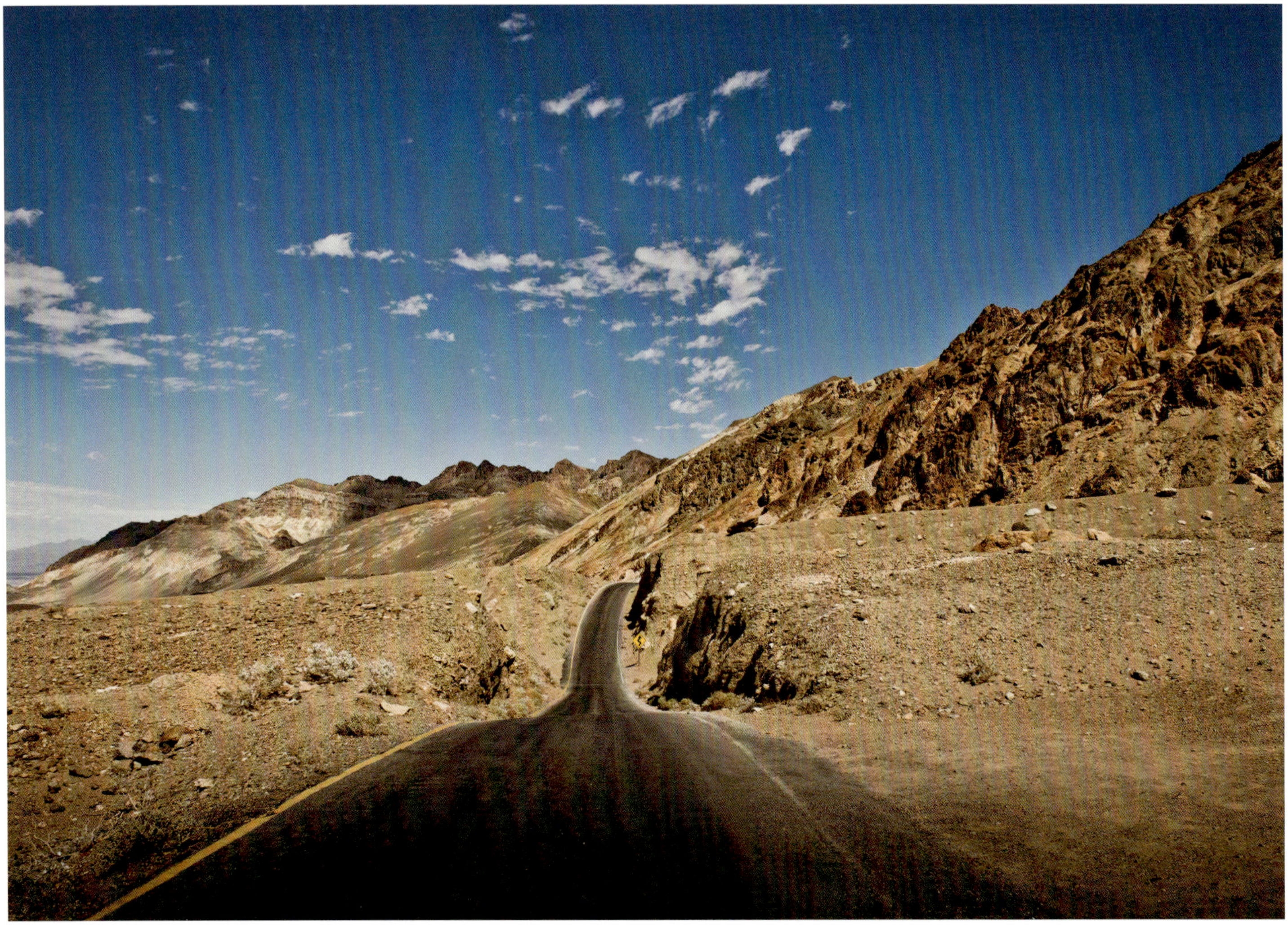

DEATH VALLEY

YOSEMITE LAS VEGAS

Auf der dritten Etappe überqueren wir die Sierra Nevada weiter nach Osten, biegen dann am Mono Lake ab und rollen durch das trockene Owens Valley nach Süden. Über die Bergkette der Panamint Mountains geht die Reise nun erneut nach Osten – hier ist dann endgültig der Eintritt in eine der trockensten und heißesten Gegenden der Erde geschafft: Das legendäre Death Valley zieht mit seiner eigentümlich unerbittlichen Atmosphäre jeden Besucher in seinen Bann. Bei Pahrump verlassen wir den Bundesstaat Kalifornien und rollen für eine Stippvisite ins benachbarte Nevada. Die weltberühmte Casino- und Entertainment-Stadt Las Vegas ist das Ziel dieser landschaftlich äußerst eindrücklichen Etappe.

—

On the third stage, we continue eastward across the Sierra Nevada, turning off at Mono Lake and rolling south through the parched Owens Valley. Heading across the Panamint Mountains, the journey turns eastward once more, ultimately bringing us to the entrance of one of the driest and hottest places on earth. The legendary Death Valley draws all who visit under its spell with its singularly remorseless atmosphere. We leave the state of California near Pahrump and head on into neighboring Nevada for a flying visit. The world-famous casino and entertainment city of Las Vegas is the final destination of this stage, characterized by unspeakably imposing scenery.

815 KM • 8 STUNDEN // 506 MILES • 8 HOURS

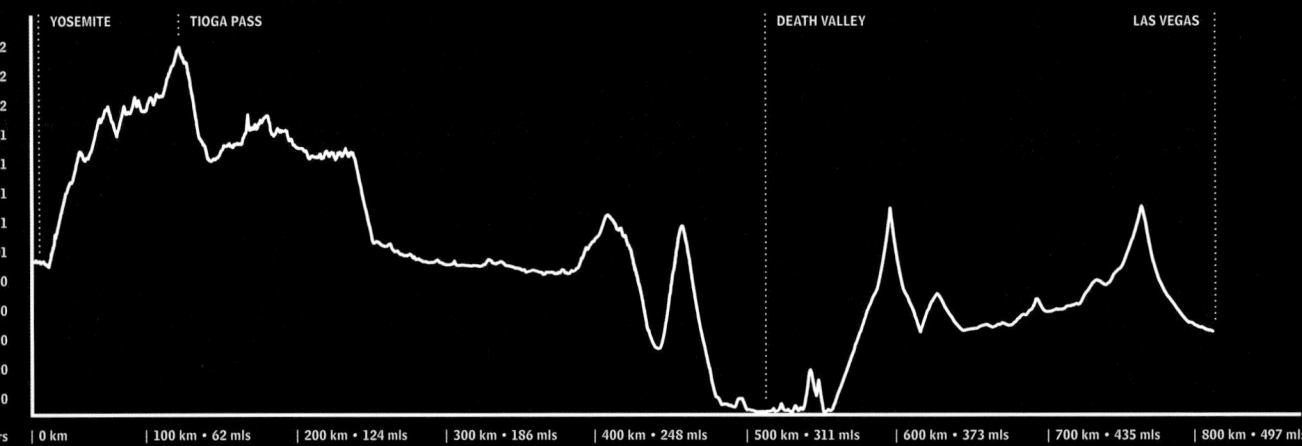

LAS VEGAS
PALM SPRINGS

662 KM • 8 STUNDEN // 411 MILES • 8 HOURS

Leichte Kopfschmerzen, die Sonne sticht viel zu hell in die schmerzenden Augen. In Las Vegas sind solche Komplikationen ganz normal ... Der Helikopter steht mit laufendem Rotor auf einem Heliport mitten in der Stadt. Ringsum die bizarren Türme der Casinos und Hotels, leuchtend, vulgär, maßlos.

—

Slight headache; the sun is far too bright for the aching eyes. In Las Vegas, this kind of complication is completely normal ... The helicopter stands on a heliport in the center of town with its rotor turning. All around are the bizarre towers of the casinos and hotels, gleaming, vulgar, excessive.

HOTELS

MANDALAY BAY
3950 S LAS VEGAS BLVD
LAS VEGAS, NV 89119
WWW.MANDALAYBAY.COM

29 PALMS INN
73950 INN AVE
TWENTYNINE PALMS, CA 92277
TEL. +1 760 367 3505
WWW.29PALMSINN.COM

Vollgas! Aus dem weichen Wummern der Rotorblätter und dem hellen Sirren der Turbine wird ein infernalisches Hämmern, ein brutales Jaulen. Plötzlich verschiebt sich der Horizont um ein paar Meter, der Pilot stabilisiert die ganze Fuhre kurz, dann wirft er die Maschine hoch in die Luft. Beängstigend nach vorne geneigt steigt die Maschine nach oben, befreit sich aus der Anziehungskraft der Türme ringsherum. Die roten Spitzhüte der Minarett-Türme des Excalibur leuchten auf, über die mystisch-schwarze Pyramide des Luxor laufen ganze Lichtreflex-Kaskaden, dann brettert der Helikopter voll durchgeladen über den dreiflügeligen Koloss des Mandalay und seine pastellblaue Badelandschaft. Von hier oben sieht Las Vegas, dieses frivole Unterhaltungs-Geschwür mitten in einer puritanischen, bußfertigen Wüste, auf einmal ganz friedlich aus. Autos auf Schachbrett-Straßen, ein blinkender Jahrmarkt verschmolzen mit einer Stadt, im Westen und Süden die endlosen Aneinanderreihungen explosionsartig wuchernder Wohngebiete.

Plötzlich legt sich der Vogel in eine magenumkehrende Schräglage, beschleunigt sämig und sägt dann nach Osten los. Nach wenigen Minuten ist Las Vegas unter uns Geschichte, die Wüste hat uns wieder. Der Pilot deutet nach links, krächzend und übersteuernd kommt seine Stimme aus den Kopfhörern: „Hoover Dam!" Wir starren in die angedeutete Richtung, bis die Pupillen ausgetrocknet sind, sehen aber außer einem dunklen Halbmond im sandbeigen Grund nichts weiter. Das muss Lake Mead sein, der Stausee im Colorado River, an dessen Tropf Las Vegas hängt. Zielstrebig und kerzengerade poltert die Maschine dahin, inzwischen keine 100 Meter über dem Boden. Aus dieser Höhe ist jeder Dornstrauch zu sehen. Und dann ist da auf einmal dieser Schatten in der weiten Fläche voraus. Eine dunkle Linie. Ein schmaler Riss im Boden. Das eben noch munter schnatternde Intercom-Gespräch

Hit it! The gentle hum of the rotor blades and the light buzz of the turbine become an infernal hammering, a brutal howl. Suddenly, the horizon shifts by a few meters, the pilot briefly stabilizes the whole affair then throws the machine up into the air. Alarmingly tilted forward, it climbs skyward, freeing itself from the pull of the towers surrounding it. The red spires of the Excalibur's minarets flash, cascades of reflected light flow along the mystic black of the Luxor's pyramid then the helicopter hurtles at full pelt over the three-wing colossus of the Mandalay and its pastel-blue bathing complex. From up here, Las Vegas, this frivolous ulcer of entertainment in the middle of a repentantly puritanical desert, somehow looks quite peaceful. Cars drive along chess-board streets in this strange fusion of city and twinkling fairground. To the west and south are the endlessly proliferating rows of booming residential areas.

Suddenly, the bird tilts over at a belly-churning angle, accelerates languidly and chatters its way eastward. A few minutes later, Las Vegas is history for us; we're back in the grips of the desert. The pilot points to the left. Through the headphones, his voice sounds raspy and over-amplified: "Hoover Dam!" We stare in the direction indicated until our pupils are all dried out. But aside from a dark half-moon in the sandy-beige ground, we can't see anything. That must be Lake Mead, the reservoir on the Colorado River that provides Las Vegas with its intravenous liquid lifeline. The machine rumbles on a determined beeline toward it, now less than 100 meters above the ground. We can see every bit of thorn scrub from this height. And then all of a sudden there's this shadow on the vast expanse ahead – a dark line, a narrow crack in the earth. The lively conversation we were just having over the intercom comes to an abrupt halt and all occupants gaze expectantly forward. "The Grand Canyon," announces the pilot solemnly, at which point the helicopter

> Klein wie eine Ameise, kaum vor der enormen Felswand wahrzunehmen, bewegt sich ein winziger Punkt mit zappelnden Flügeln an der Ostkante des Grand Canyon entlang. Du hältst die Luft an. Fassungslos.

> As tiny as an ant, barely noticeable against the enormous wall of rock, a miniscule dot with juddering wings is moving along the eastern edge of the Grand Canyon. You hold your breath in stunned amazement.

bricht schlagartig ab, alle Insassen schauen gespannt nach vorn. „Grand Canyon", sagt der Pilot dann feierlich, und in diesem Moment schießt der Helikopter über die Kante. Unter uns sackt der Erdboden weg. Hunderte von Metern tief. Ein dunkelroter Abgrund aus Fels, ganz weit unten der schmale Strich des Colorado River. Dein Magen dreht sich schlagartig in einem Anfall von Höhenangst, die Eingeweide stürzen ins Bodenlose. Gestandene Männer stoßen entsetzt die Luft aus und die Damen kreischen. Nur der Pilot schmunzelt kaum merklich, dann deutet er zur anderen Seite des Canyons: „Dort drüben, da ist ein anderer Hubschrauber!" Wieder suchst Du beinahe vergeblich – bis Dir klar wird, dass Dein Gefühl für Entfernungen in diesem Abyss völlig falsch justiert ist: Klein wie eine Ameise, kaum vor der enormen Felswand wahrzunehmen, bewegt sich ein winziger Punkt mit zappelnden Flügeln an der Ostkante des Grand Canyon entlang. Du hältst die Luft an. Fassungslos.

Regelrecht euphorisiert fällt die Truppe zurück in Vegas aus dem Hubschrauber, trabt zögernd zu den Autos auf dem Parkplatz nebenan. Mal sehen, wie lange der Ritt zum Hoover Dam mit Bodenhaftung dauert. Ob wir uns die Fahrfreude mit der Vogelperspektiven-Aktion verdorben haben? Wohl kaum: Wir entscheiden uns für eine kleine Rundfahrt durchs Valley of Fire nordwestlich von Las Vegas, und eine Stunde später stehen wir auf der gigantischen Staumauer aus über zweieinhalb Millionen Kubikmetern Stahlbeton, die in einem rund 200 Meter breiten Tal den Colorado River zu einem 640-Quadratkilometer-See abklemmt. Aus dem Helikopter hätte das vermutlich niedlich gewirkt. Erst mit den Füßen auf dem heißen Beton, nur wenige Meter von den archaischen, riesenhaften Wassereinlauftürmen entfernt, wird einem das absurde Ausmaß des Hoover Dam klar. Beinahe andächtig steuern wir den Elfer zurück auf den Highway 93 nach Südwesten. Der Hoover Dam ist der östlichste Punkt unserer Reise, ab hier beginnt der

shoots over the edge. The earth disappears from beneath us – hundreds of meters deep. A dark-red chasm, and far below at the bottom is the narrow strip of the Colorado River. My belly promptly starts churning in an attack of vertigo, my guts plunging into the abyss. Grown men gasp and women squeal, only the pilot smiles quietly and almost imperceptibly to himself then points to the other side of the canyon: "There's another helicopter over there!" You search again, almost in vain – until you realize that your feel for distance in this chasm is all wrong. As tiny as an ant, barely noticeable against the enormous wall of rock, a miniscule dot with juddering wings is moving along the eastern edge of the Grand Canyon. You hold your breath in stunned amazement.

It is with utter euphoria that the group tumbles out of the helicopter back in Las Vegas, before traipsing hesitantly to the cars on the parking lot next door. Let's see how long the ride to the Hoover Dam takes by road. Have we ruined the fun of driving with this bird's eye stunt? Not at all. An hour later we're standing on the gigantic dam wall made from more than two-and-a-half million cubic meters of reinforced concrete, sealing off a width of around 200 meters across the Colorado River valley to create a 640 square-kilometer lake. From the helicopter, it would probably have looked quaint. It's not until your feet are on the hot concrete, just a few meters from the huge,

LAS VEGAS

HOOVER DAM

GRAND CANYON

Vor allem aber scheint der Straßenplaner hier nicht wie auf den letzten 200 Meilen alleine mit dem Lineal gearbeitet, sondern sich völlig entspannt der Topografie hingegeben zu haben: Ein schmales Straßenband kurvt um Hügel herum und durch ausgetrocknete Flussbetten hindurch.

Most noticeably, however, is that the road planners here didn't work exclusively with a ruler, as has been the case for the last 200 miles. They appear instead to have happily dedicated themselves to the local topography. A narrow band of road wends its way around hills and through dried-out river beds.

lange Weg zurück zum Pazifik. Es ist eine Reise, die erfinderisch macht – irgendwie muss man sich auf den beinahe bizarr langweiligen Geradeaus-Etappen ja unterhalten. Wir versuchen es beispielsweise mit skurrilen Ortsnamen: Wer auch immer als Erster wieder ein wunderliches Kaff entdeckt, kann Punkte sammeln.

Gigantische Solarfelder blinken in der Sonne, ein paar Meilen die Straße hinunter liegt passenderweise die globale Metropole „Searchlight" – das Entdecken der Verbindung ist auf jeden Fall für einen Punkt gut. „Cal-Nev-Ari" klingt irgendwie israelisch, ist aber einfach nur eine Abkürzung für die in der Nähe liegende Staaten-Grenze: California-Nevada-Arizona. Gut aufgepasst? Punkte!

„Palm Gardens" könnte auch „Etikettenschwindel" heißen. Um das kleine Straßen-Gitter aus frischem Asphalt sammeln sich zwar ein paar Einfamilien-Häuser und heimelig im Nichts der Wüste erschlossene Bauplätze, aber weit und breit finden sich keine Palmen. Wohin die Leute hier wohl ihre Kinder in die Schule schicken? Nach „Bagdad", „Cadiz" oder „Sibirien" drüben in Kalifornien vielleicht? Egal, unsere Punkteliste wird ganz von selbst immer länger. In „Twentynine Palms" geben wir das Spiel endgültig auf, hier bietet sich endlich ein etwas weniger verzweifelter Zeitvertreib.

archaic water inlet towers, that you appreciate the absurd dimensions of the Hoover Dam. Almost reverently, we turn the 911 back onto Highway 93, heading southwest. The Hoover Dam is the easternmost point of our journey. This is the start of the long road back to the Pacific. It's a journey that makes you quite inventive – you have to keep yourself entertained on the almost bizarrely boring straight sections. We try, for instance with comical place names: Points go to the first one to discover a whimsically worded backwater. Massive expanses of solar panels glint in the sunlight. A few miles down the road is the fittingly named global metropolis of "Searchlight" – spotting that connection is definitely worth a point. "Cal-Nev-Ari" sounds somehow Israeli, but is simply short for the nearby state borderline: California-Nevada-Arizona. Were you paying attention? Points!

"Palm Gardens" could also be called "False Labeling". There may well be a few single-family homes gathered around the small street grid of freshly laid asphalt and building plots under development nestled in the nothingness of the desert, but as far as the eye can see, there are no palm trees whatsoever. Where do these people send their children to school? To "Bagdad", "Cadiz" or "Siberia" over in California perhaps? No matter, our score sheet is getting longer as we speak. In "Twentynine Palms", we give up

VALLEY OF FIRE

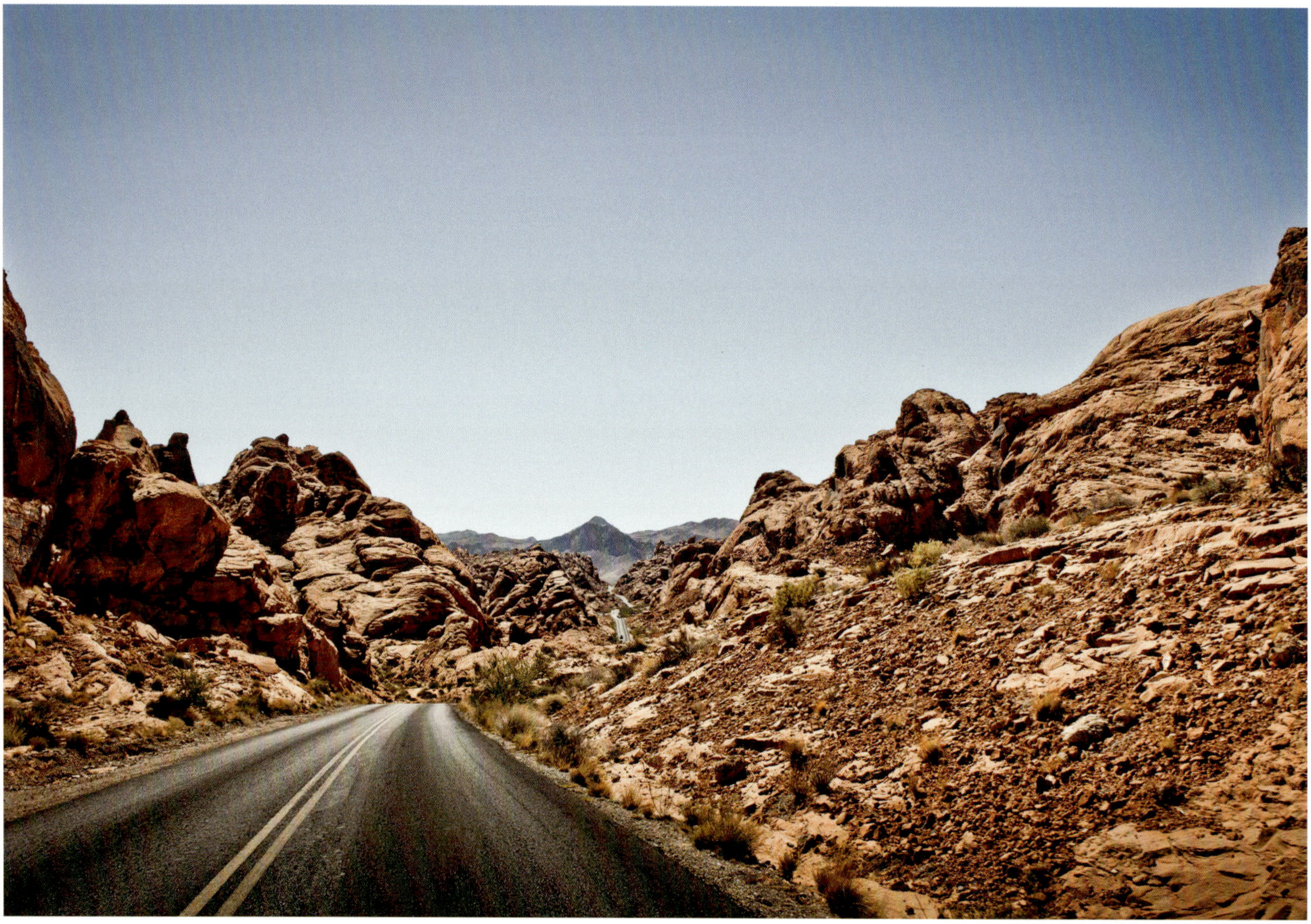

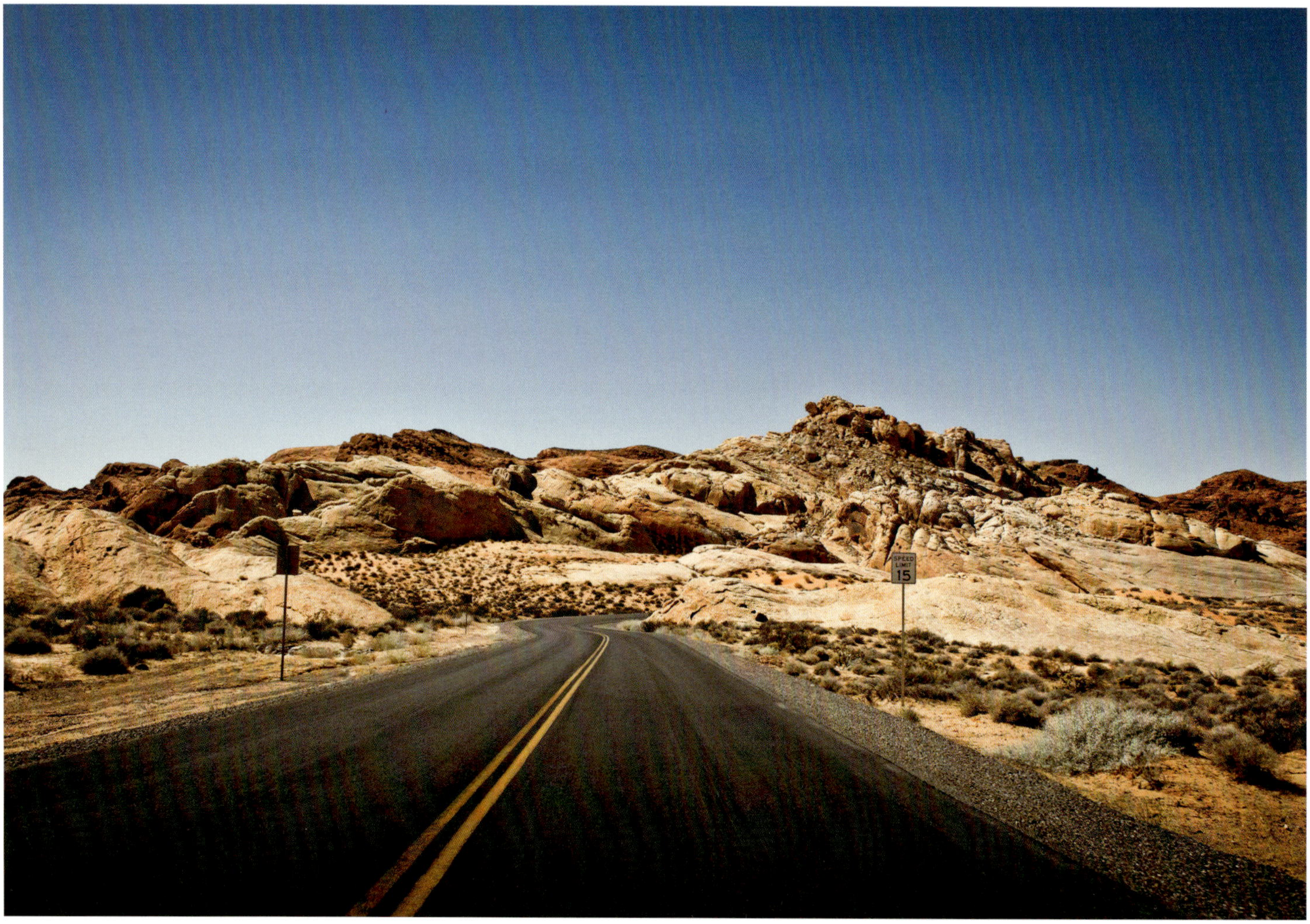
SPEED LIMIT 15

VALLEY OF FIRE

VALLEY OF FIRE

Südlich der Wüstenstadt mit ihren rund 30 000 Einwohnern liegt der Joshua Tree National Park, der mit seinen Felsformationen aus Riesenmurmeln und den charakteristischen Yucca-Palmen eine ganz eigentümliche Atmosphäre hat. Vor allem aber scheint der Straßenplaner hier nicht wie auf den letzten 200 Meilen alleine mit dem Lineal gearbeitet, sondern sich völlig entspannt der Topografie hingegeben zu haben: Ein schmales Straßenband kurvt um Hügel herum und durch ausgetrocknete Flussbetten hindurch. Selbstverständlich haben wir uns für diese Etappe das Album „Joshua Tree" der irischen Band U2 eingepackt; die Bluesharp bei „In God's Country" passt mit ihrem irrlichternden Sound ganz famos zu den Meilen im Park. Dabei scheinen nicht alle Bewohner oder Besucher des Nationalparks ein Faible für sendungsbewusste Iren zu haben: Der Josua-Baum auf dem Plattencover, die wohl berühmteste Palmlilie der Welt, soll einem Akt des Vandalismus zum Opfer gefallen sein. Wer weiß, vielleicht hat auch Bono höchstpersönlich die Motorsäge ausgepackt?

Erst am südlichen Ende hören wir auf die stille Botschaft der Joshua Trees, die mit ihren ausgestreckten Armen einer Mormonen-Legende zufolge wie der biblische Josua ins gelobte Land nach Westen zeigen: Über den Interstate 10 segeln wir in Richtung Abend – das erste Mal auf dieser Reise, dass wir uns mit einer dieser ultrabreiten Interkontinental-Autobahnen abgeben. Endlich hat uns die Mojave-Wüste doch weichgekocht.

Palm Springs ist ein angenehmer Schock. Musik, Essen, Menschen, Swimming Pools. Seit Las Vegas haben wir das beinahe vergessen. Sind uns beinahe nicht sicher, ob uns eine warme Strömung doch wieder zurück ins Nichts spült. Aber dann landet das Auto im Neon-Licht. Und wir bestellen uns ein Bier.

on the game once and for all, having finally found a slightly less desperate pastime. South of the desert town of around 30 000 inhabitants is the Joshua Tree National Park, with its highly distinctive atmosphere created by giant rock formations and the characteristic yucca plants for which it is named. Most noticeably, however, is that the road planners here didn't work exclusively with a ruler, as has been the case for the last 200 miles. They appear instead to have happily dedicated themselves to the local topography. A narrow band of road wends its way around hills and through dried-out river beds. It goes without saying that we packed the album "Joshua Tree" by Irish band U2 especially for this part of the trip. The ghostly sound of the blues harp on "In God's Country" is absolutely perfect for the miles through the park. However, not all of the national park's inhabitants and visitors appear to be quite as taken by the Irish activists: The joshua tree on the album cover, surely the world's most famous yucca, allegedly fell victim to an act of vandalism. Who knows, maybe it was Bono himself who took a chainsaw to it?

It's not until the southern end of the park that we stop to listen to the silent message of the joshua trees. According to a Mormon legend, their outstretched arms pointed the way westward to the Promised Land for the biblical Joshua. We sail along Interstate 10 into the evening – the first time on this trip that we have yielded to one of these ultra-wide intercontinental highways. The Mojave Desert has finally worn us down.

Palm Springs is a pleasant shock. There's music, food, people, swimming pools – we had almost forgotten about all that since leaving Las Vegas. We're not actually sure that a warm current isn't going to wash us back into nothingness. But then the car finds its way into the neon light, and we order ourselves a beer.

HOTELS

HOPE SPRINGS RESORT
68075 CLUB CIR DR
DESERT HOT SPRINGS, CA 92240
TEL. +1 760 329 4003
WWW.HOPESPRINGSRESORT.COM

RESTAURANT

PAPPY & HARRIET'S
53688 PIONEERTOWN RD
PIONEERTOWN, CA 92268
TEL. +1 760 365 5956
WWW.PAPPYANDHARRIETS.COM

WORKSHOP KITCHEN + BAR
800 N PALM CANYON DR
PALM SPRINGS, CA 92262
TEL. +1 760 459 3451
WWW.WORKSHOPPALMSPRINGS.COM

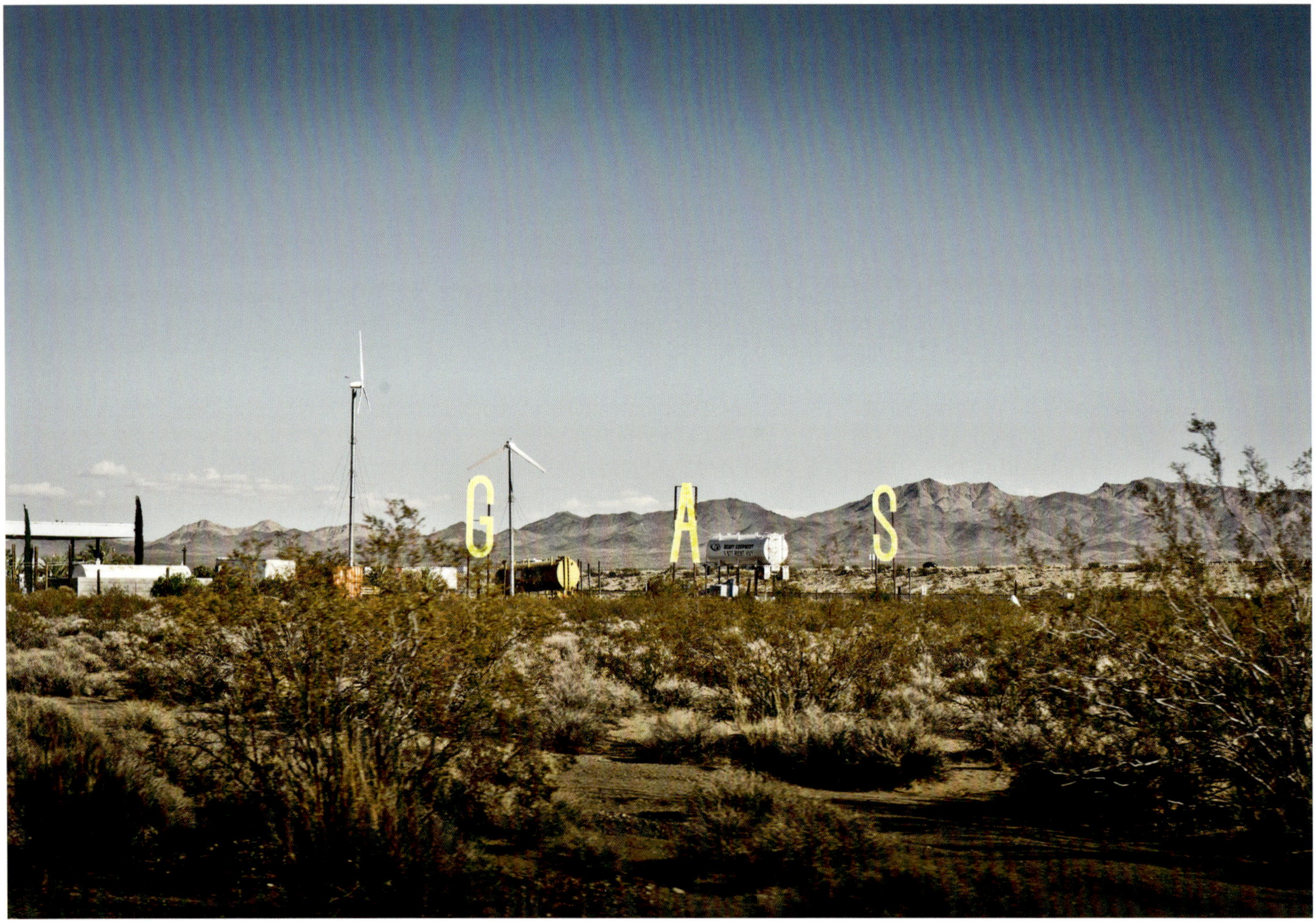
GAS

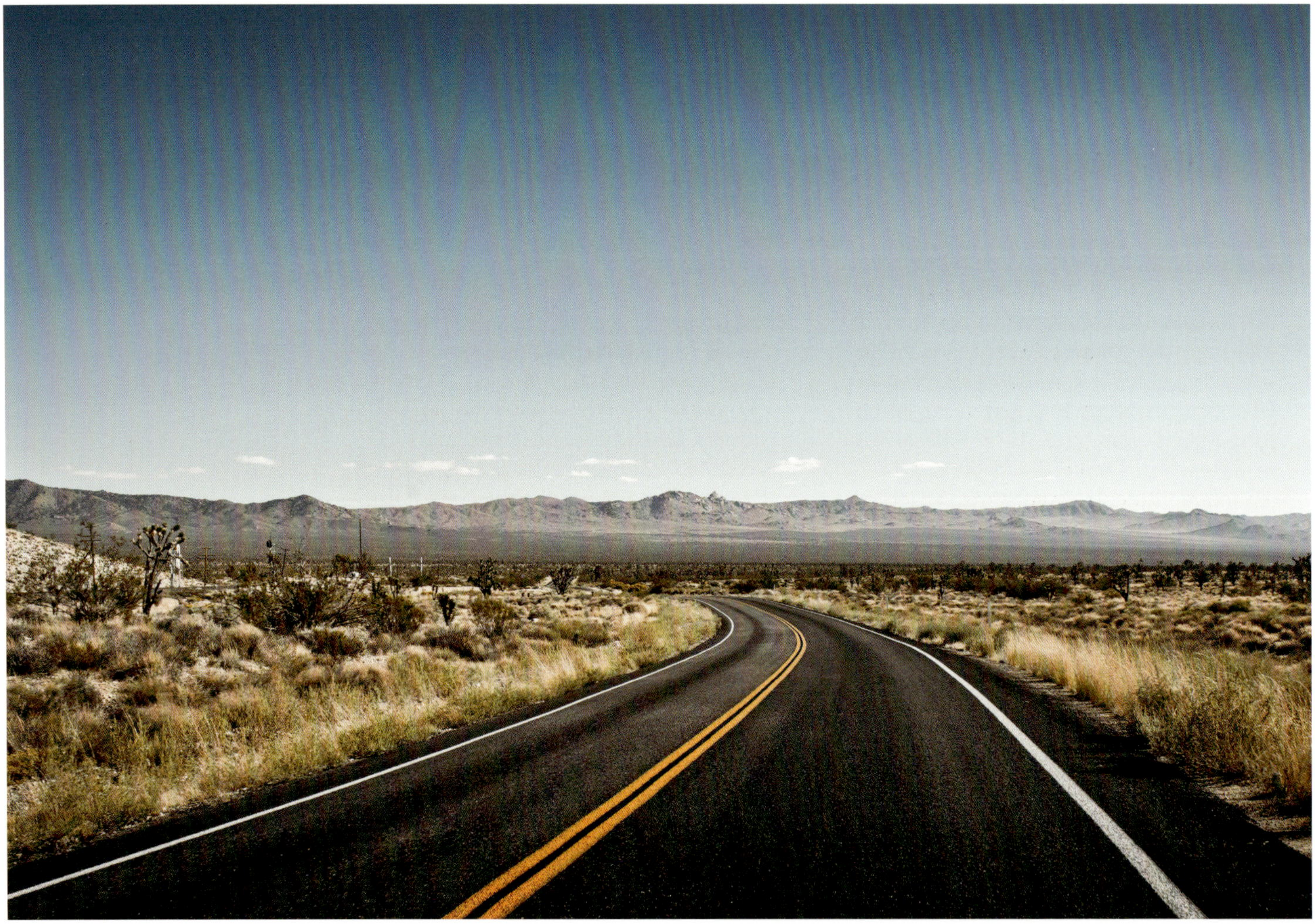

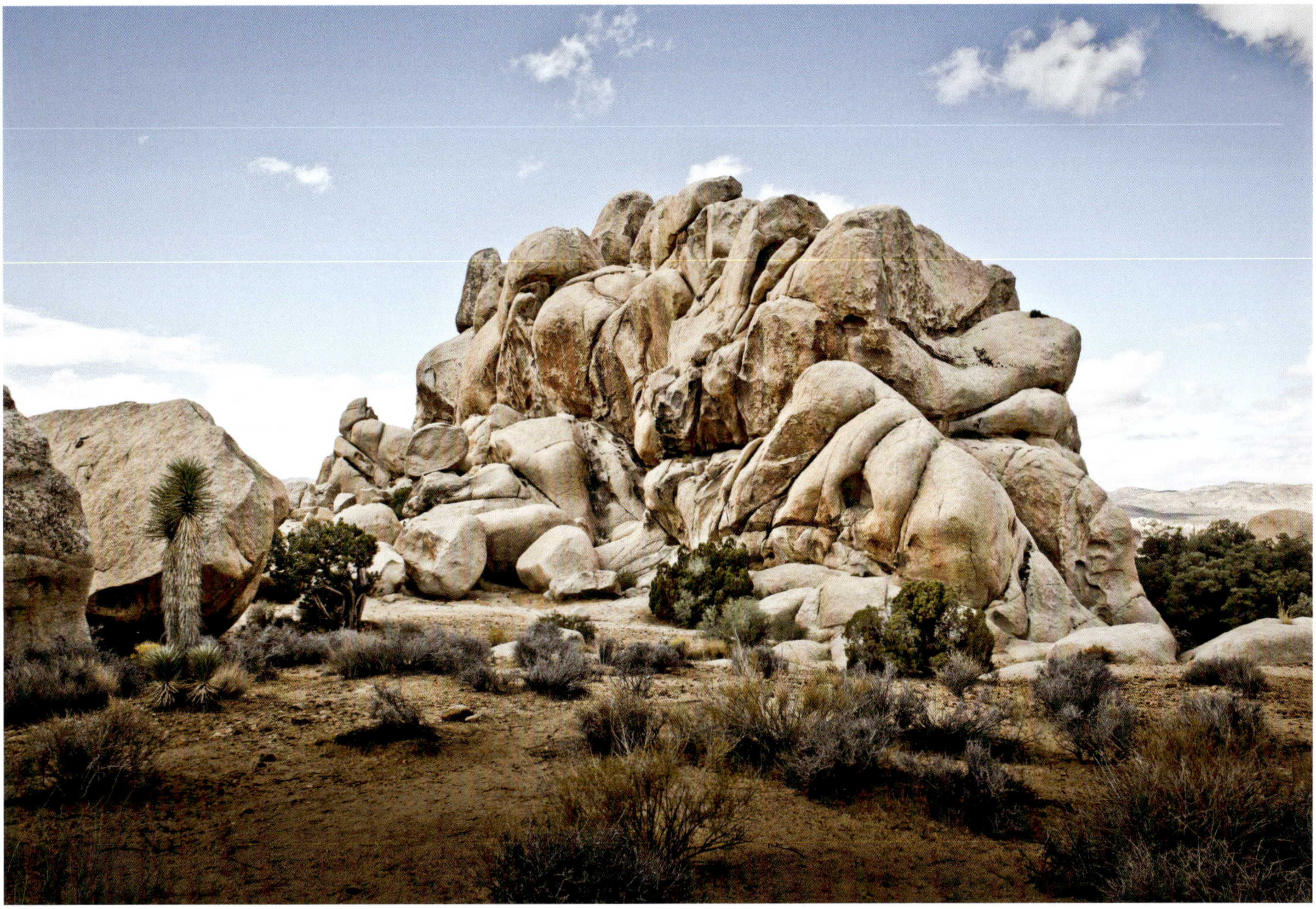

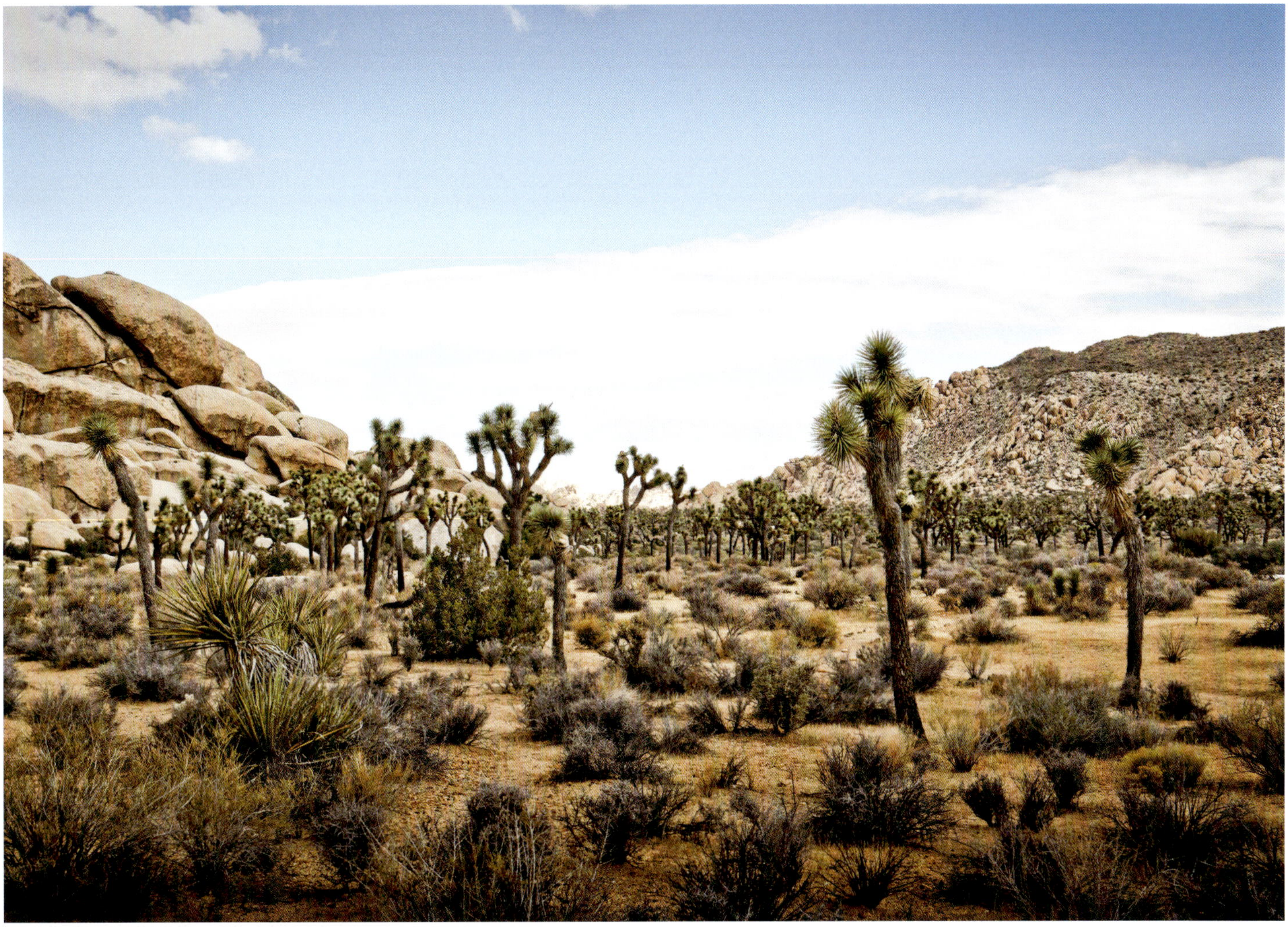

UNITED STATES
POST OFFICE
PIONEERTOWN, CALIFORNIA
SHERIFF'S OFFICE

LAS VEGAS PALM SPRINGS

Am Hoover-Staudamm erreichen wir den östlichsten Punkt unserer Reise. Das gigantische Bauwerk staut seit den 1930er-Jahren den Colorado River und versorgt so in einer völlig lebensfeindlichen Umgebung gleich drei Bundesstaaten mit Elektrizität und Wasser. Ab Boulder City verläuft unsere Route beinahe direkt nach Süden, bei Bullhead City haben wir wieder die Grenze nach Kalifornien erreicht und setzen die Fahrt durch die Mojave-Wüste fort. Bei Twentynine Palms verlassen wir die großen, schnurgerade verlaufenden Wüsten-Highways für einen Umweg durch den Joshua Tree National Park. Die Straße schwingt sich hier durch eine faszinierende und abwechslungsreiche Landschaft; unser Etappen-Ende erreichen wir im verträumt-mondänen Palm Springs.

—

We reach the most easterly point of our journey at the Hoover Dam. The colossal structure has been shoring up the Colorado River since the 1930s, supplying no fewer than three states with electricity and water from utterly hostile surroundings. As of Boulder City, our route runs almost directly southward, bringing us once more to the border of California at Bullhead City, from where we continue the drive through the Mojave Desert. At Twentynine Palms, we leave the main, arrow-straight desert highway for a detour through Joshua Tree National Park. The road sweeps through a fascinating and widely diverse landscape, bringing us to the end of this stage in the wonderfully glamorous Palm Springs.

662 KM • 8 STUNDEN // 411 MILES • 8 HOURS

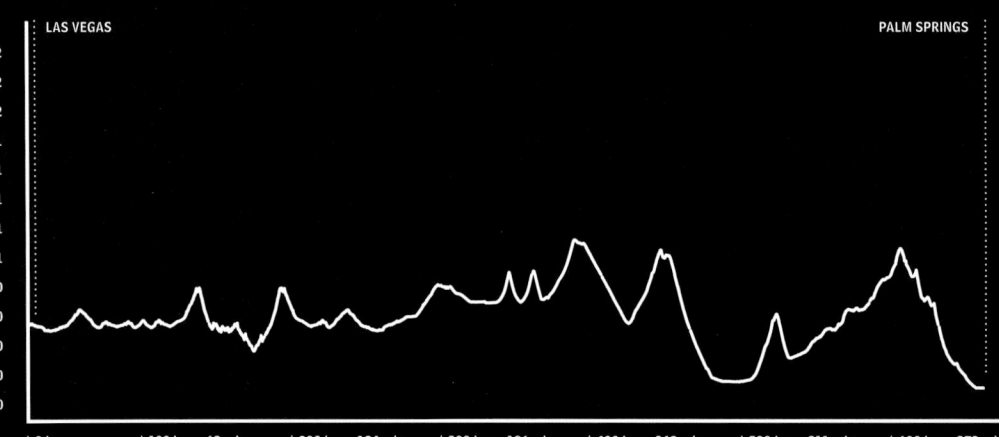

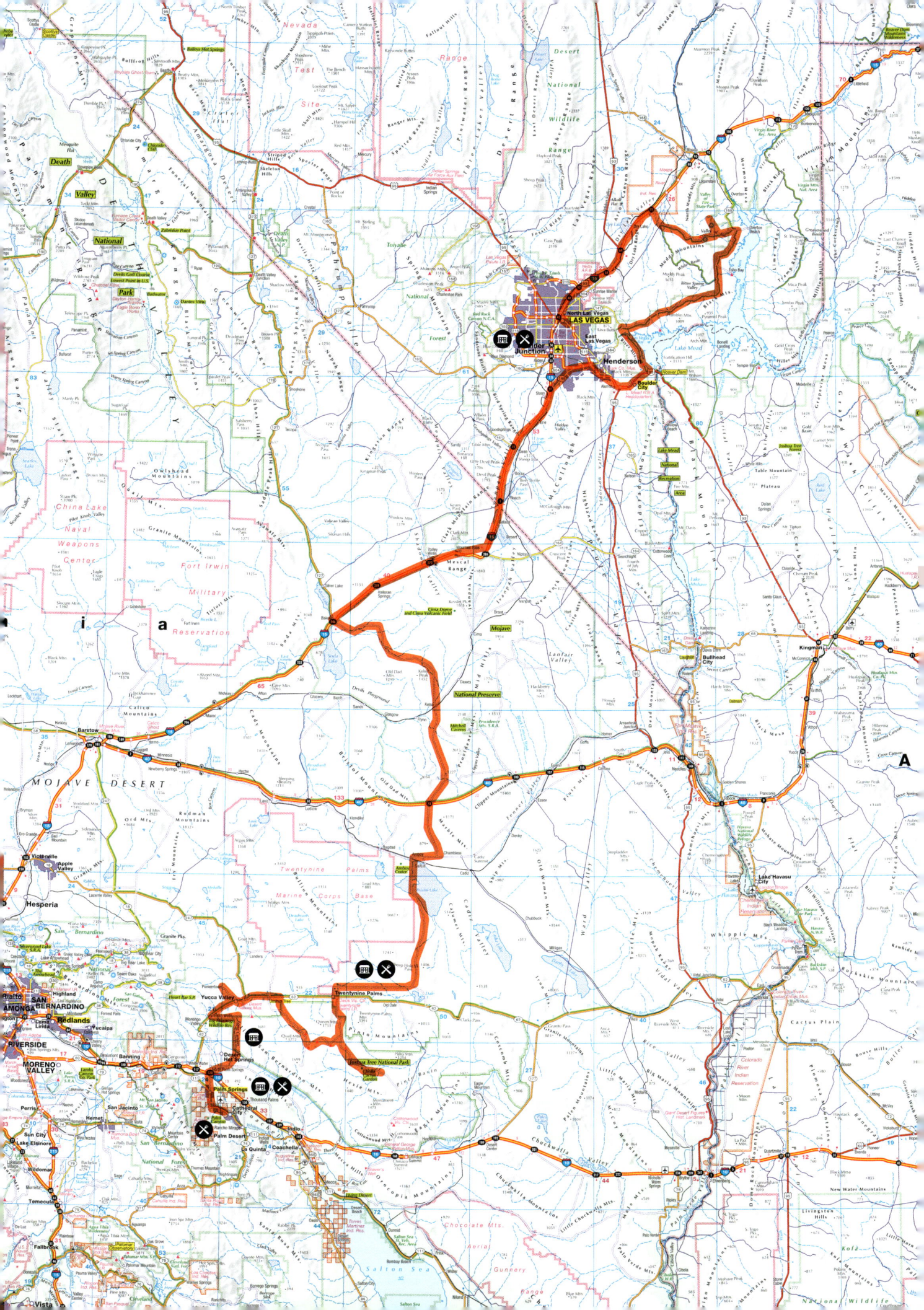

PALM SPRINGS
LOS ANGELES

756 KM • 10 STUNDEN // 470 MILES • 10 HOURS

Aufwachen in Palm Springs. Die Wüste steckt Dir noch in den Knochen. Zieht vor Deinem inneren Auge vorüber, hat Dich müde und monoton gemacht, gleichzeitig ist das Unterbewusstsein überschwemmt mit Emotion. Geahnte Nahtod-Erfahrung.

—

Waking up in Palm Springs, the desert is still deep in your bones. It flits across your mind's eye; you found it monotonous and tiring, but at the same time, your subconscious is overflowing with emotion. It has the feel of a near-death experience, complete solitude, absolute boredom.

Vollkommene Einsamkeit. Absolute Langeweile. Und gleichzeitig die Erfahrung, dass gerade in der Monotonie zum Zerreißen gespannte Trance steckt, die Begegnung mit kompromissloser Lebensfeindlichkeit vibrierende Lebenslust auslöst und dass Langeweile nur geduldig kultiviert werden muss, um sich in einen satten Ich-Jetzt-Zustand zu wandeln. In Palm Springs kondensiert die während der letzten vielen hundert Meilen gesammelte Weisheit plötzlich. Die Stadt hätte auch von Psychiatern erfunden werden können: Eine Stadt zwischen Es und Ich, zwischen Zivilisation und Wildnis, zwischen Vollgas und Tank leer.

Drüben, hinter den San Jaquinto-Bergen tobt das moderne Kalifornien, zwei Stunden auf dem Interstate 10, und Du bist in Los Angeles. Prall, schnell, böse, zuckersüß, wham-bamm. Oben in Idlewild hat das ländliche Kalifornien dagegen einen ruhigen Rhythmus gefunden. Und nur ein paar Meilen zurück in der Wüste ist ein Tag ein paar Millionen Jahre lang. Genau an dieser Schnittstelle liegt Palm Springs. Die Stadt hat schon immer Aussteiger aus Los Angeles angezogen, die sich nicht so recht von der Großstadt trennen konnten oder wollten, Elvis Presley hatte hier eine Villa, Frank Sinatra einen Swimmingpool. Ein klein wenig Normalität, ein wenig Auszeit von der Schallgeschwindigkeit des Entertainment-Business, ein wenig kleinbürgerliche Privatsphäre. Und vielleicht ein wenig Ekstase, stoned mit dem Motorrad in die Wüste rausfahren.

Vielleicht ist Palm Springs also eine Stadt, in der Zerrissenheit einen erträglichen Fixpunkt findet. Oder ist Palm Springs die pure Unentschlossenheit? Wir entscheiden uns. Lassen Los Angeles noch einmal zappeln und fahren Kurs Südost, zum Salvation Mountain. Die quietschbunte Kunst-Installation bei Calipatria wurde vom Aussteiger Leonard Knight angefertigt, ihre kein bisschen subversive Botschaft passt jetzt

Yet you also experience that, within this monotony, there is a stupor stretched to breaking point that releases a vibrant lust for life in the face of such uncompromising hostility. That boredom simply has to be patiently cultivated for it to turn into a deep sense of self in the here-and-now. All the wisdom gathered over the hundreds of miles behind us suddenly condensed when we reached Palm Springs. The city could have been founded by psychiatrists. It is a city somewhere between me and it, between civilization and wilderness, between foot-down and empty.

Over there, cavorting behind the San Jaquinto Mountains, is modern-day California. Two hours on Interstate 10 and you're in Los Angeles – bursting at the seams, fast, wicked, sickly sweet, wham-bam. Up in Idlewild, on the other hand, rural California has found a peaceful rhythm. And just a few miles back in the desert is a day several million years long. Palm Springs lies right on this transition point. This town has always attracted Los Angeles dropouts, who couldn't or didn't really want to tear themselves away from the big city. Elvis Presley had a villa here, Frank Sinatra a swimming pool. It offers a little bit of normality, a short timeout from the sonic speed of the entertainment business, a piece of bourgeois privacy. And maybe even a bit of ecstasy – riding into the desert on a motorbike, stoned out of your face.

Perhaps Palm Springs is a town where conflict finds a bearable anchor. Or is Palm Springs nothing more than plain vacillation? We take our decision, leave Los Angeles to thrash around a little longer and embark on a southeasterly course to Salvation Mountain. The gaudy art installation near Calipatria was created by drop-out Leonard Knight, its slightly subversive message now somehow fitting: God is Love. Although you have to go in search of Him – Salvation Mountain is not on any of the

In Palm Springs kondensiert die während der letzten vielen hundert Meilen gesammelte Weisheit plötzlich. Die Stadt hätte auch von Psychiatern erfunden werden können: Eine Stadt zwischen Es und Ich, zwischen Zivilisation und Wildnis, zwischen Vollgas und Tank leer.

All the wisdom gathered over the hundreds of miles behind us suddenly condensed when we reached Palm Springs. The city could have been founded by psychiatrists. It is a city somewhere between me and it, between civilization and wilderness, between foot-down and empty.

irgendwie: God is Love. Man muss Gott freilich suchen, der Salvation Mountain liegt nicht an einer der großen, vielbefahrenen Routen. Aber die göttliche Liebeserklärung gehört vielleicht gerade hierher, und auch auf nicht-religiöse Reisende übt dieser tief ernsthafte Kitsch eine seltsam beruhigende Wirkung aus.

Was natürlich auch am nahe gelegenen Salton Sea liegen kann, der eine fast apokalyptische Geschichte von Schuld und Sühne erzählt: Kaliforniens Schicksal hängt am Wasser, soviel ist klar, und die Bemühungen der Planer, das Wasser des Colorado River für die Entwicklung Kaliforniens nutzbar zu machen, haben bereits um 1905 eine Katastrophe ausgelöst. Beim Bau eines Überlaufs bricht der Damm, innerhalb von zwei Jahren füllt der so lebensnotwendige Fluss das Becken des Imperial Valley. Erst 1907 kann der Colorado River wieder vollständig in sein altes Bett zurückgegraben werden – im Salton-Bassin lässt die menschengemachte Katastrophe aber einen rund 1000 Quadratkilometer großen See zurück, der in den folgenden Jahrzehnten immer salziger wird. Biblische Tragik, ein XXL-Diorama wie aus dem alten Testament. Südlich des Sees fahren wir auf dem Highway 78 nach Westen, langsam bleibt die archaische Wüste im Rückspiegel zurück. Je näher man der Küste kommt, desto freundlicher wird das Land, die Berge duften plötzlich wieder nach Kräutern und Blumen.

major, high-traffic routes. But perhaps this is exactly where the declaration of holy love belongs. This deeply serious piece of kitsch manages to exercise a strangely calming effect even on non-religious travelers.

This could, of course, also be due to the nearby Salton Sea, which has a tale to tell of almost apocalyptic guilt and atonement. The fate of California depends on water, that much is clear, and planners' efforts to make the water of the Colorado River usable for California's development resulted in catastrophe back in 1905. The dam burst during construction of an overflow and the life-giving river ran into the dry lake bed in Imperial Valley for two whole years. It wasn't until 1907 that the course of the Colorado River was dug fully back into to its old bed. The manmade catastrophe left behind a 1000 square-kilometer lake in the Salton Basin, which became increasingly saline over the decades that followed. It was a tragedy of biblical dimensions – a supersized diorama like something from the Old Testament. South of the sea, we head

PALM SPRINGS

WORLD'S BIGGEST DINOSAURS GIFT STORE

God is Love. Man muss Gott freilich suchen, der Salvation Mountain liegt nicht an einer der großen, vielbefahrenen Routen. Aber die göttliche Liebeserklärung gehört vielleicht gerade hierher, und auch auf nicht-religiöse Reisende übt dieser tief ernsthafte Kitsch eine seltsam beruhigende Wirkung aus.

God is Love. Although you have to go in search of Him – Salvation Mountain is not on any of the major, high-traffic routes. But perhaps this is exactly where the declaration of holy love belongs. This deeply serious piece of kitsch manages to exercise a strangely calming effect even on non-religious travelers.

Pferde grasen auf den Koppeln einsam gelegener Ranches. Übermütig turnt die Straße durch Santa Ysabel und Ramona, vorbei an Escondido – und dann wird die Luft plötzlich salzhaltig, feucht, schwitzend. Bei Encinitas rollt das Auto am Strand aus. Regelrecht fassungslos blinzeln wir in die Sonne und schauen fasziniert aufs Meer hinaus: Hallo Pazifik, lange Zeit nicht gesehen! Mit den bloßen Füßen im Sand und einer steifen Brise Seewind in den Haaren verfolgen wir die Surfer in der mahlenden Brandung. Wilde Gestalten, die wie Treibgut auf dem stahlgrauen Wasser wirken und konzentriert den Rhythmus der Wellen studieren. Dann und wann scheint eine der kleinen Figuren da draußen regelrecht zu explodieren, paddelt aus Leibeskräften, dicht dahinter steigt eine massige Flut aus dem Meer. Dann ein Schwung, die Figur steht auf dem Brett und die Welle packt zu. Gischtender Wahnsinn, eine brechende Röhre, Vollwaschgang.

Interessant, wie wenig das Klischee vom schönen, sexy, wilden Surfer mit der Realität korrespondiert: Wie nasse Hunde stolpern vom Seewasser zerfressene und von der Sonne verbrannte Kreaturen zurück an den Strand, mit zerfetzen Füßen und fleckiger Haut, strohigen Haaren und leerem, hypnotisiertem Blick. Surfen scheint wenig mit den bunt strahlenden Bildern der Adrenalin-Industrie tun zu haben, sondern eher etwas mit einer archaischen Rausch-Kultur.

west on Highway 78, the ancient desert slowly fading in the rear-view mirror. As you near the coast, the land becomes noticeably more pleasant – the mountains are once more scented with plants and flowers, and horses graze in the paddocks of secluded ranches. The road winds its way cheerfully through Santa Ysabel and Ramona, past Escondido – and then the air suddenly becomes salty, humid, sweltering. The car comes to a halt at the beach in Encinitas. We blink into the sun in amazement and stare out over the ocean in fascination – hi there, Pacific. Long time no see! Standing barefoot in the sand, with a stiff sea breeze in our hair, we watch the surfers in the crashing breakers. These are wild shapes, looking like flotsam on the steely gray water, and carefully studying the rhythm of the waves. Now and then, one of the tiny figures out there seems virtually to explode, paddling for all his might with a massive wall of ocean rising up behind him. Then comes a surge of momentum, the figure is standing up on the board and the wave strikes – foaming insanity, a breaking pipe, complete wipeout.

It's interesting how little the cliché of handsome, sexy, wild surfers corresponds with the reality. Chewed up by the ocean and scorched by the sun, these creatures stagger back to the beach like wet dogs, with tattered feet and blotchy skin, hair like straw and an empty, hypnotized look on their

SALVATION MOUNTAIN

SALVATION MOUNTAIN

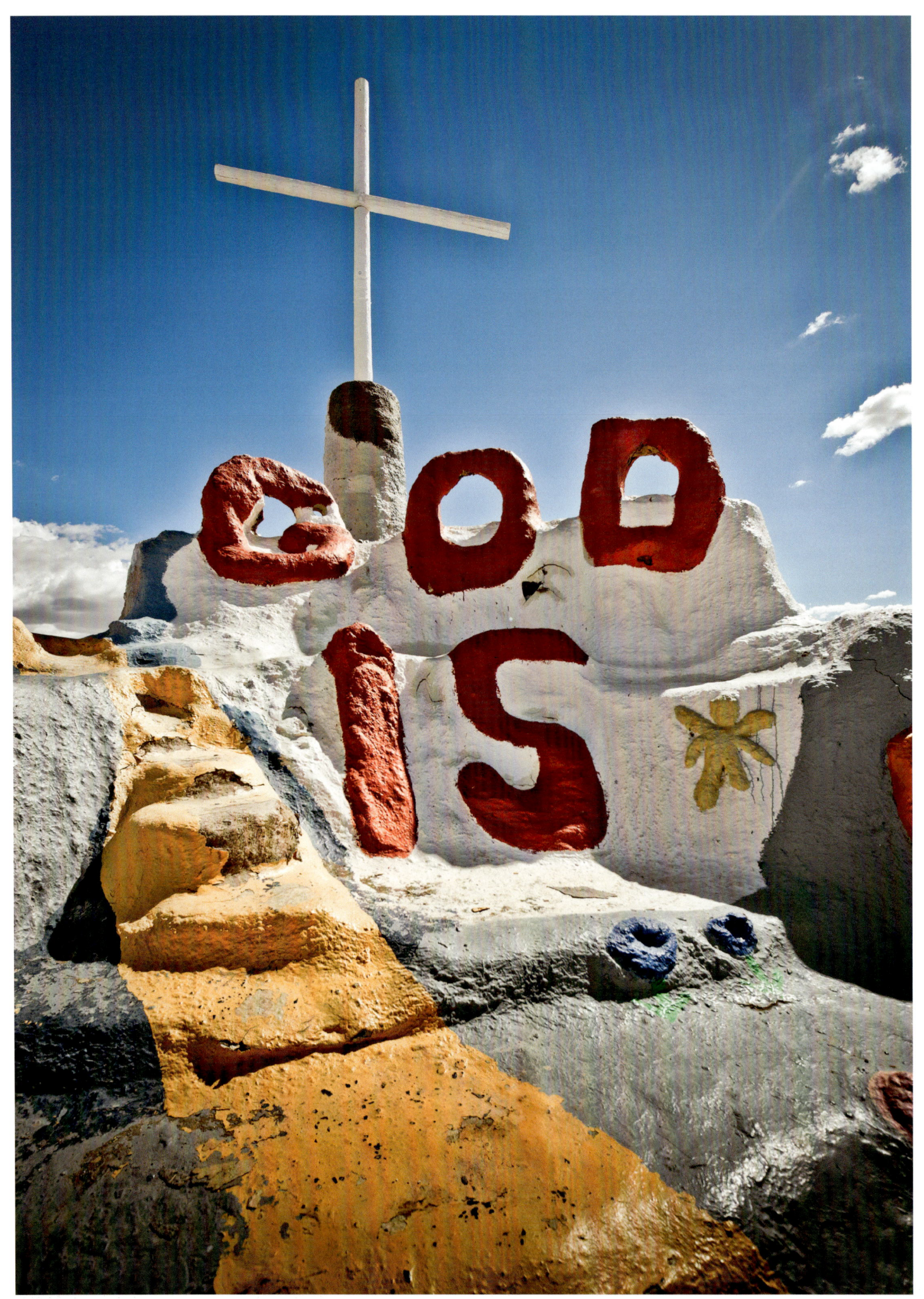

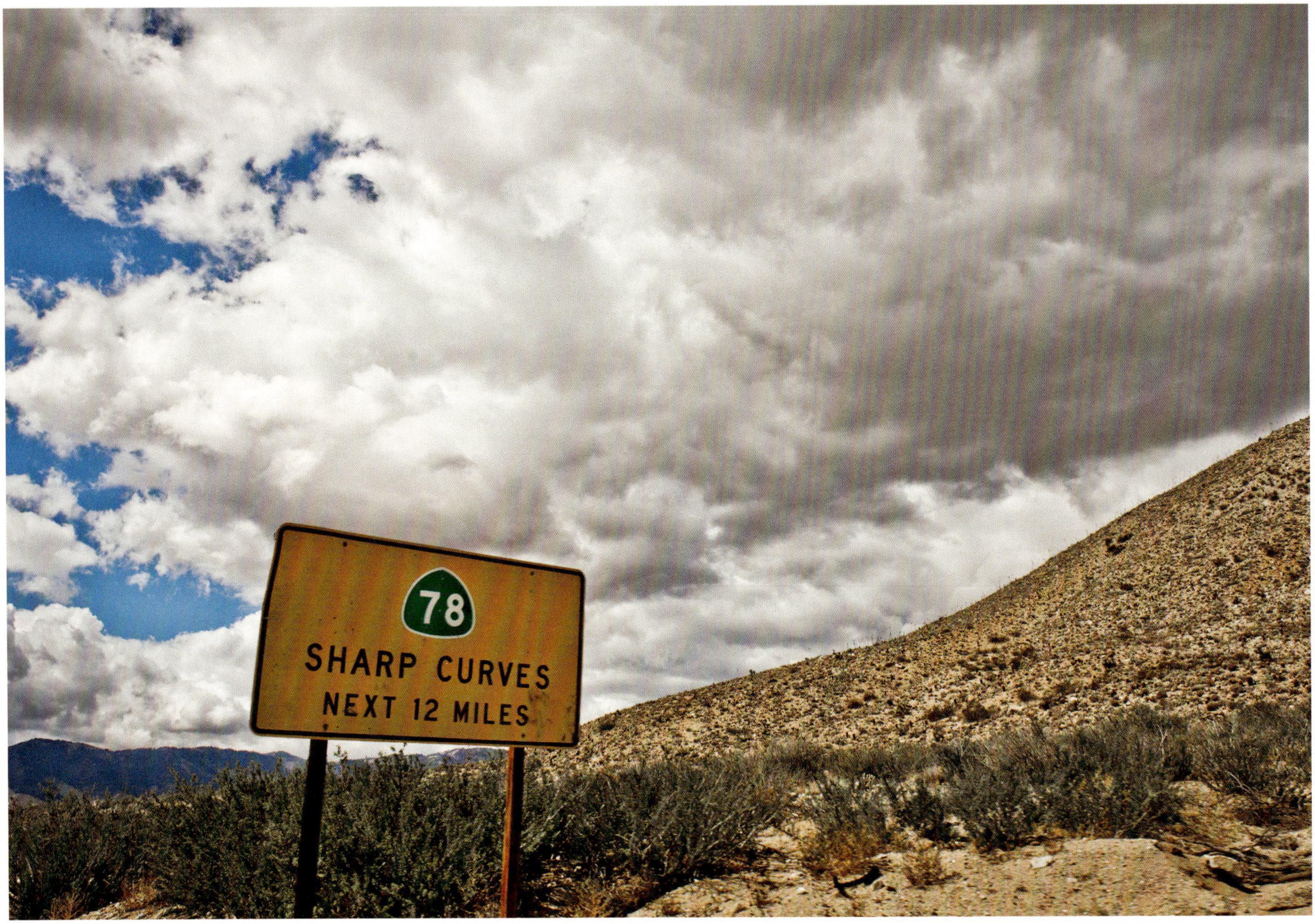
78
SHARP CURVES
NEXT 12 MILES

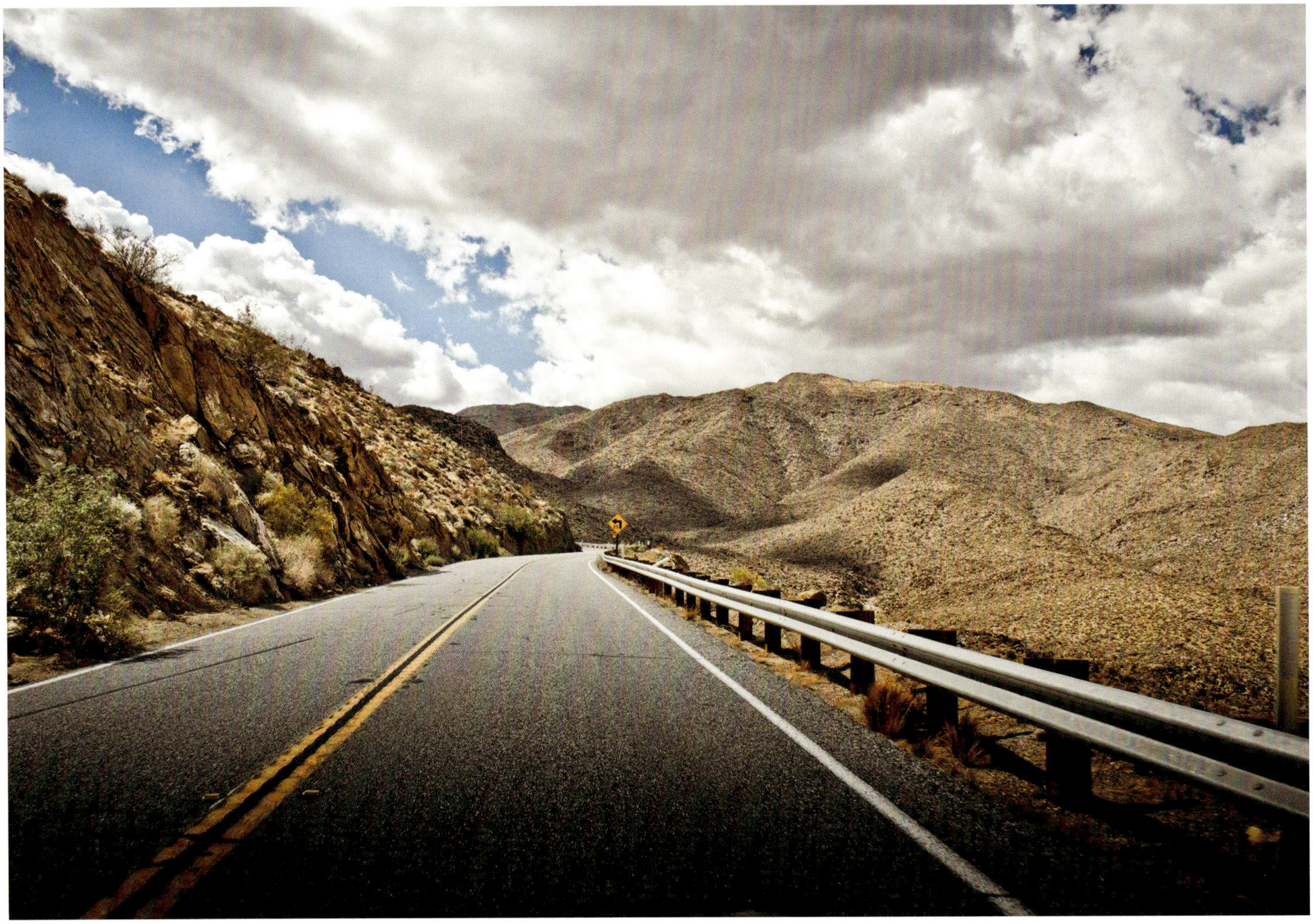

Keine Rücksicht auf Verluste, Drohgebärden gegenüber Fremden, klare Hackordnung auf dem Wasser. Gerade deshalb für uns Meilenfresser und Straßensurfer so spannend. „Curves" und „Waves" – das ist in letzter Konsequenz wesensverwandt. Es gibt Leute, die mit einem Automatik-Van von A nach B fahren, die Landratten. Und es gibt uns. Die Soulful Drivers. Keine Erklärung notwendig.

Nach einem befriedigenden Abstecher in die Seafood- und California Kitchen-Restaurants geht es weiter nach Norden. So langsam mischt sich in jede zurückgelegte Meile eine nagende Wehmut: Bald wird die Reise zu Ende sein. Bald. Desillusioniert lassen wir uns auf dem Interstate 5 durch Carlsbad und Oceanside treiben, bei Dana Point wechseln wir zurück auf den Highway No. 1. Laguna Beach, Newport Beach, dann die gigantischen Container-Terminals von Long Beach. Der Hafen von Los Angeles, ein kochender Umschlagplatz, der nicht auf diesem Planeten zu liegen scheint, sondern an einem Wasser-Wurmloch in andere Universen.

Rüber nach Redondo Beach, dann streunt das Auto im Stop-and-Go-Zuckeltrab durch die netten Straßen von Manhattan Beach. Augen zu und am Flughafen vorbei – bevor wir Kalifornien endgültig verlassen, haben wir noch eine letzte Tour vor. Den Kurven-Refill, eine letzte Zugabe, bevor die Band endgültig von der Bühne geht. Nachschlag, Nachtisch. Wir lassen uns mit dem brandenden Verkehr der Metropole durch L.A. Downtown schieben, biegen dann in Richtung Pasadena ab und nehmen im letzten Moment die Ausfahrt zum Highway No. 2: Kurven in den San Gabriel-Bergen. Hochmütige Europäer, die an das Märchen von den langweiligen Straßen in den USA glauben, erleben hier Bekehrung, Taufe und Wiedergeburt: Der Angel Crest Highway ist eine Legende, 60, 70, 80 Meilen von komplett anderweltigem Kurven-Irrsinn. Erst viel später rollt der Elfer wieder am südlichen Fuß der Berge aus. Leerer, hypnotisierter Blick des Fahrers. Big Wave. Wir haben sie gefunden. *In God's own Country.*

faces. Surfing seems to have less to do with the radiantly colorful images of the adrenaline industry, and more with an archaic culture of intoxication. No thought is given to casualties, threatening gestures toward strangers, a clear pecking order on the water. This is particularly fascinating to us "road surfers". Curves and waves – at the end of the day, they are two sides of the same coin. There are people who drive from A to B in an automatic van – landlubbers. And then there's us – the soulful drivers. No explanation necessary. After a welcome detour into the Seafood and California Kitchen Restaurants, we continue northward. With every mile, a gnawing melancholy slowly starts to set in – the journey will soon be at an end. Soon. Disillusioned, we wander along Interstate 5 through Carlsbad and Oceanside, turning back onto Highway No. 1 at Dana Point. Laguna Beach, Newport Beach then the gigantic container terminals of Long Beach. The port of Los Angeles is a heaving transfer site seems to stand not on this planet, but on a water-wormhole to other universes.

We cross over to Redondo Beach, before the car strays into a stop-and-go conga line through the pleasant streets of Manhattan Beach. We close our eyes as we pass the airport – we have one more tour ahead of us before we ultimately leave California. It's a curve refill, one last encore before the band finally leaves the stage – seconds or dessert, if you will.

We let the city's surging traffic push us through downtown L.A., before turning off for Pasadena and, at the last minute, taking the exit to Highway No. 2 – curves in the San Gabriel Mountains. This is where arrogant Europeans who believe in the fairytale of boring USA roads experience their conversion, baptism and rebirth. The Angel Crest Highway is a legend – 60, 70, 80 miles of completely surreal curve lunacy. It's not until much later that the 911 finally rolls back out at the southern foot of the mountain – the driver wearing an empty, hypnotized look on his face. The big wave – we found it. *In God's own country.*

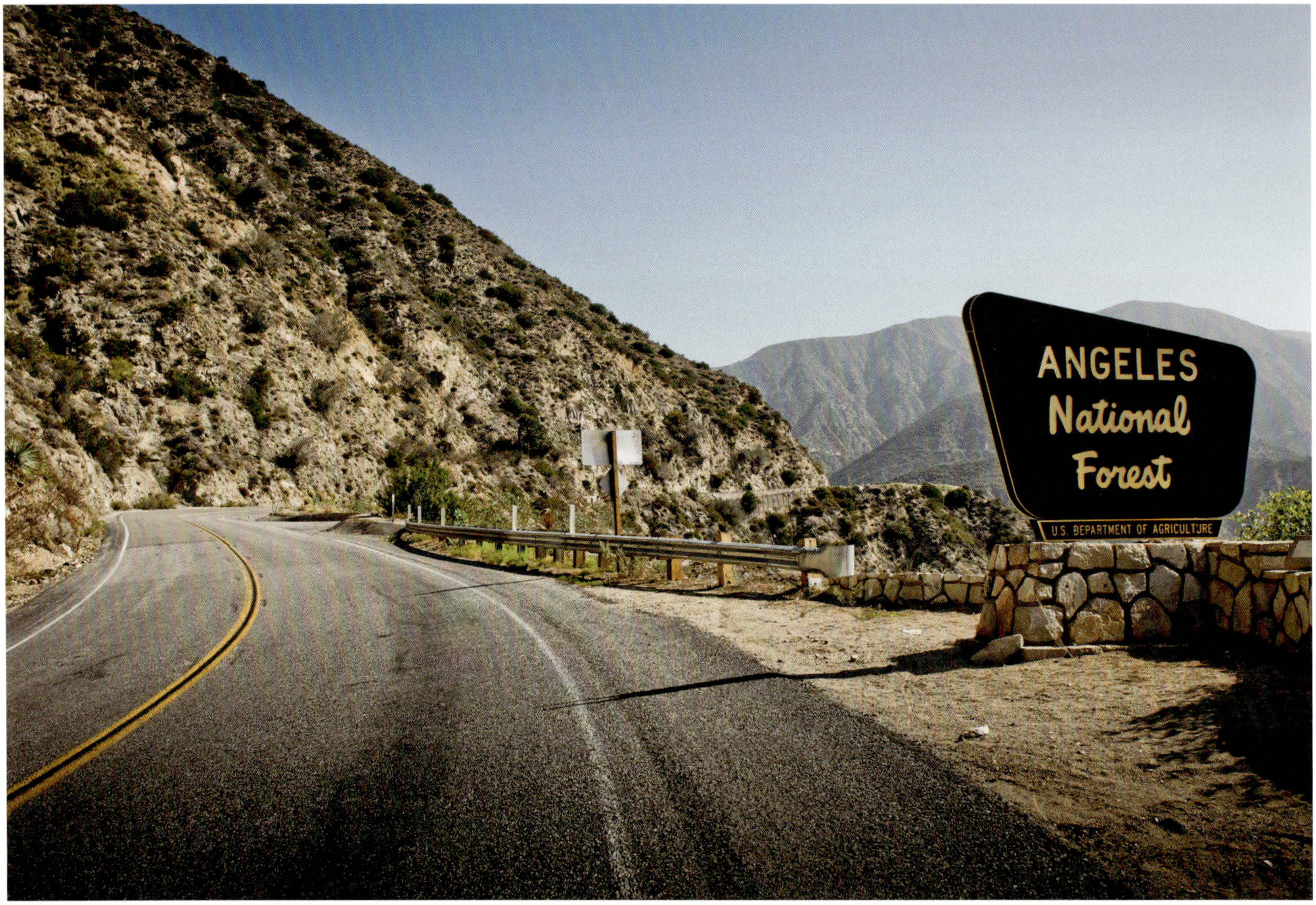
ANGELES
National
Forest
U.S. DEPARTMENT OF AGRICULTURE

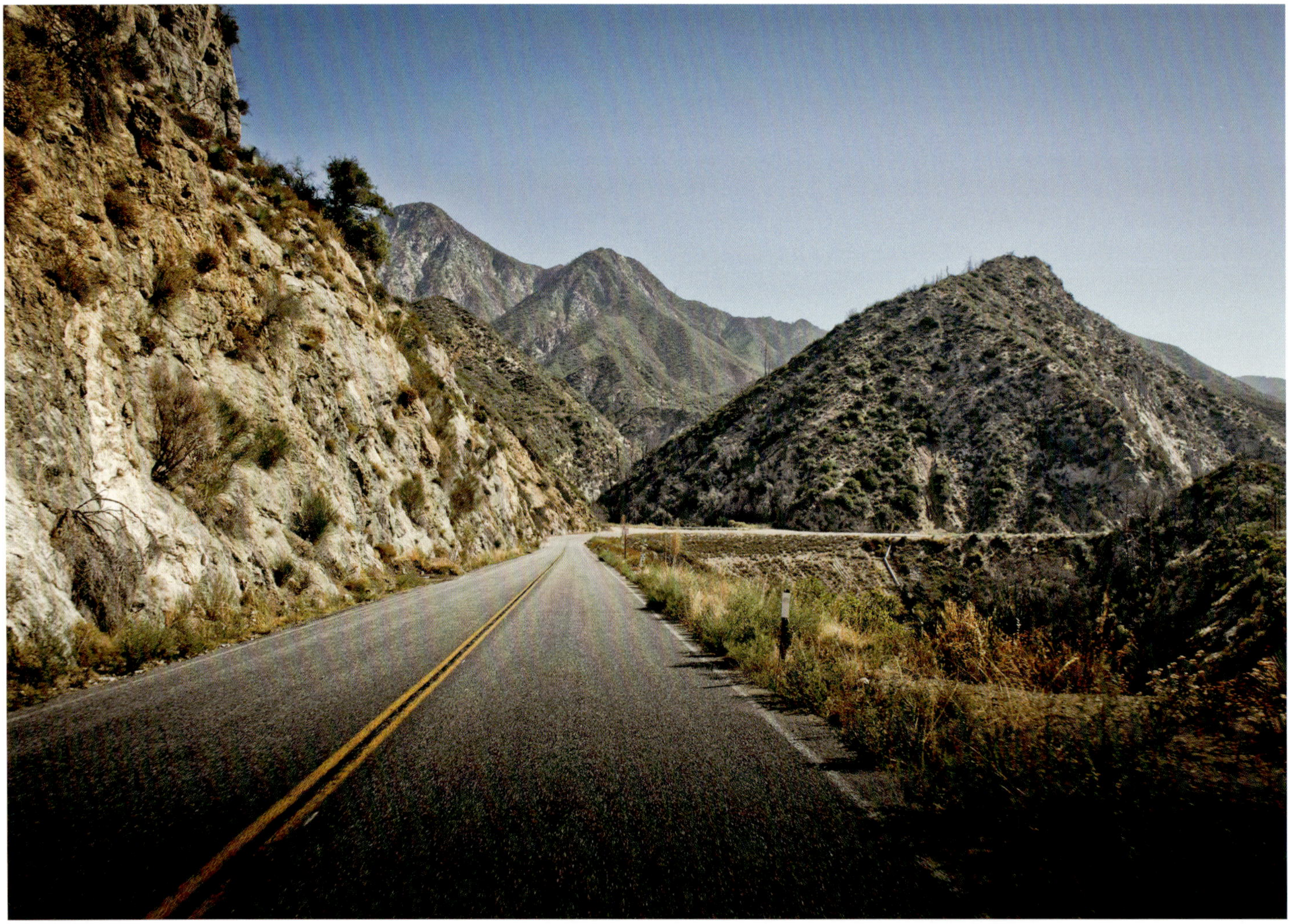

PALM SPRINGS LOS ANGELES

Die letzte Etappe unserer Reise durch den Westen der USA ist mit bizarren Sehenswürdigkeiten und wilden Landschaften äußerst spannend, das Tour-Finale wird darüber hinaus auf kurvenreichen Landstraßen gebührend gefeiert. Aus Palm Springs fahren wir zum Salvation Mountain, einer bunten Kunstinstallation mit religiöser Botschaft, streben dann über die wildromantischen San Jacinto Mountains in Richtung Westen. Bei Encinitas haben wir den Pazifik erreicht und setzen die Fahrt nun nach Norden fort. Vorbei an den besten Surf-Spots Südkaliforniens rollen wir zurück nach Los Angeles – das Ende der Kalifornien-Tour ist bereits in Sichtweite. Zum Abschied darf dann allerdings die herbe Angel Crest-Passstraße in den San Gabriel Mountains hinter Pasadena nicht fehlen: Erst ein Kurvenritt über die vielen Meilen einsamer Bergstraßen mit Ausblick auf die Metropole am Pazifik komplettiert die Tour.

—

The final stage of our journey through the west of the USA is amazing, with some bizarre sights and wild landscapes. And the tour's finale is also fittingly celebrated on some lusciously winding back roads. From Palm Springs, we drive to Salvation Mountain, a colorful art installation with a religious message, before winding our way over the ruggedly picturesque San Jacinto Mountains, heading west. We reach the Pacific at Encinitas and continue our drive northward. We head past Southern California's best surfing spots and roll on back to Los Angeles – the end of our California tour is already in sight. As a final farewell, however, we can't possible miss out the unforgiving Angel Crest mountain pass in the San Gabriel Mountains behind Pasadena. Sweeping through bend after bend along the many miles of this quiet and secluded mountain road with a view of the city on the Pacific brings the tour to a perfect close.

756 KM • 10 STUNDEN // 470 MILES • 10 HOURS

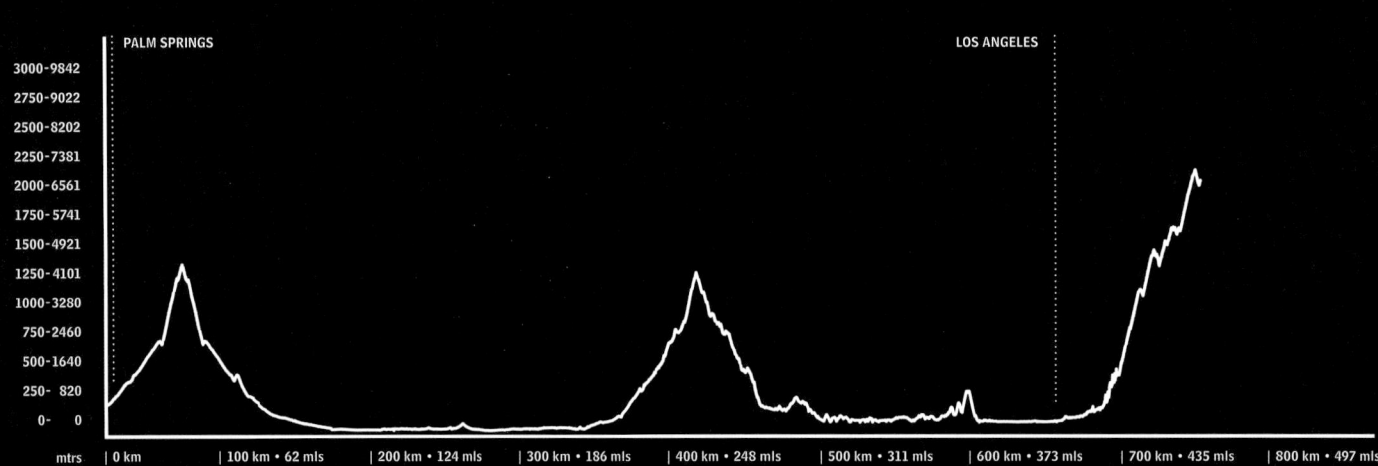

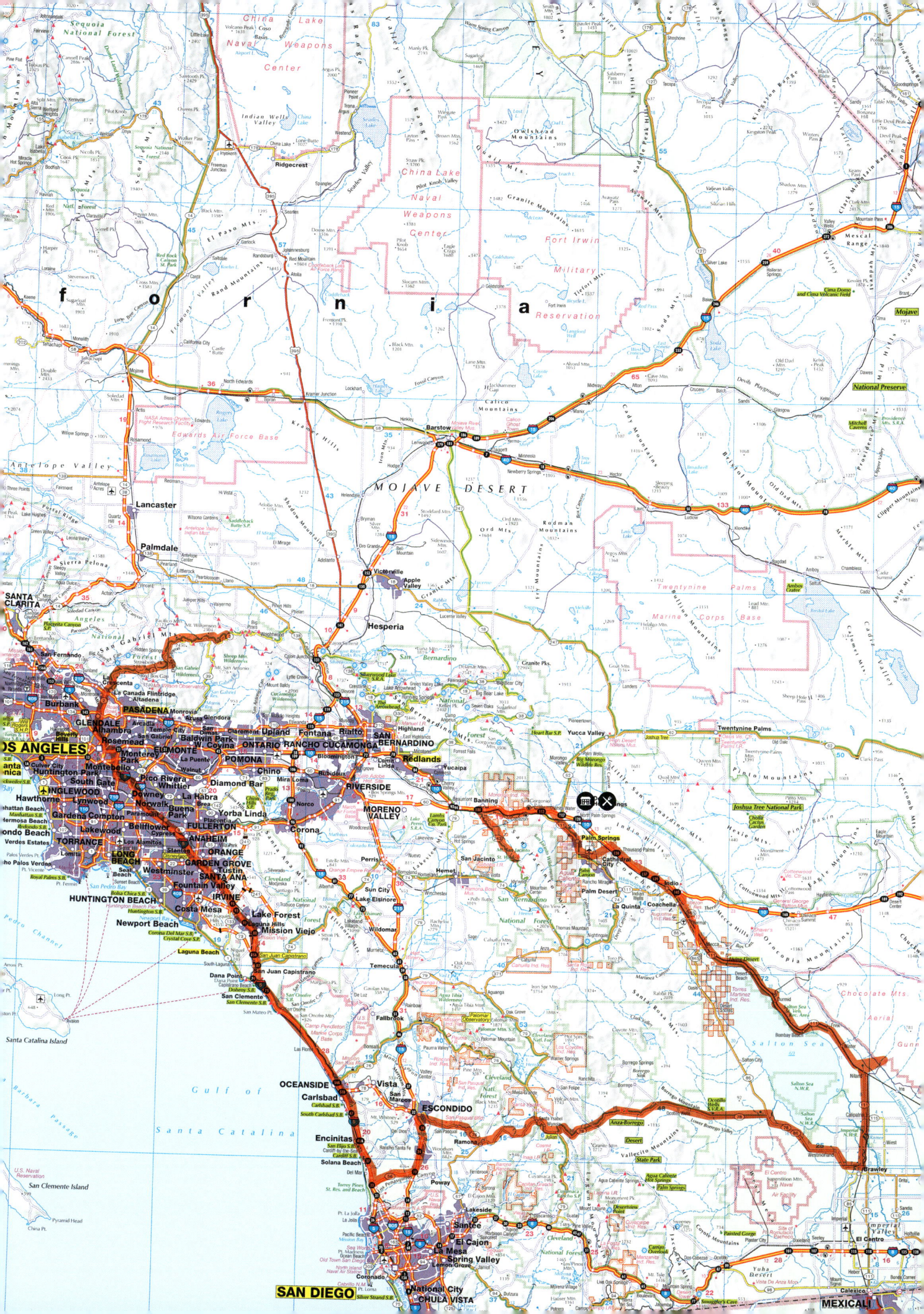

BACKSTAGE

Wir geben es zu: Auch wenn CURVES bisher immer in den Alpen oder Pyrenäen unterwegs war und seinen ganz eigenen Charakter dem kernigen Charme dieser europäischen Gebirge verdankt, hatten wir doch immer ein Auge auf Kalifornien geworfen. Einfach, weil uns in dieses atemberaubende Land an der Pazifikküste seit unserem ersten Besuch nie wieder aus dem Kopf ging. Ganz bestimmt aber auch, weil alle Roadtrips dieser Welt irgendwie nach oder durch Kalifornien gehen. Der Kern des Unterwegsseins ist die Freiheit – und auf Freiheit hat Kalifornien definitiv ein Copyright.

Unsere US-amerikanischen Leser dürfen nach diesem Geständnis jetzt für einen kurzen Moment trotzdem noch das Stars-and-Stripes-Banner eingerollt lassen – die CURVES-Macher sind allesamt Europäer und haben deshalb einen ganz eigenen Blick auf die USA, Kalifornien und dieses flüchtige, unserer Meinung nach kaum in Stereotype zu zementierende Thema „Freiheit". Europäern stechen in den USA häufig zuerst ganz naiv die Dos und Don'ts, die „No Trespassing"-Schilder ins Auge, und aus dieser Perspektive fühlt sich der Weg zur Freiheit sehr

We admit it, although CURVES has previously always concentrated on the Alps or the Pyrenees and indeed has the rugged charm of these European mountain ranges to thank for its very distinctive character, we always had our eye on California. This is simply because, since our first visit, we've never been able to get this breathtaking land on the Pacific coast out of our heads. And surely also because all road trips in this world lead to, or through, California. The core of being on the road is freedom – and California definitely holds the copyright to that.

Nevertheless, even after this confession, our American readers should keep their stars-and-stripes banners rolled up for a moment – the makers of CURVES are all European and therefore have a particular view of the USA, California and this elusive notion of "freedom", which, in our opinion, can hardly be cemented in stereotype. What Europeans notice first and foremost on a superficial level in the USA are all the dos and don'ts, the "no trespassing" signs, and, from this point of view, the road to freedom seems a very long way off. What actually fascinates us is the joy that Californians have in crazy

weit an. Was uns eigentlich fasziniert, ist die Freude der Kalifornier an verrückten Ideen, am Infragestellen von gesetzten Codes, am Experimentieren. Wer in Europa Tausende von Kilometern fährt, einfach nur um unterwegs zu sein, macht sich beinahe verdächtig. In den USA werden Soulful Drivers verständnisvoll und begeistert begrüßt. Vermutlich, weil die alte Neugier der Siedler nach dem Land hinter dem Horizont immer noch im kollektiven Bewusstsein steckt. Freiheit ist also die individuelle Lust des Sich-Treiben-Lassens – und dieser Lust haben wir uns bei der Produktion zu CURVES Kalifornien hemmungslos hingegeben. Sechzig Jahre nachdem ein junger Schauspieler namens James Dean in seinem kleinen, puristischen Porsche auf der Suche nach dem Herzschlag der Freiheit durchs Herz Kaliforniens tobte, haben wir etwas ähnliches mit dem neuen Porsche 911 gemacht – und dabei sowohl unseren inneren James Dean von der Leine gelassen als auch die begeisternde Liebesaffäre der Kalifornier mit Porsche erlebt. Kaum zu glauben, wie gut dieses ingeniöse, sehr deutsche Auto zum California-Lifestyle passt. In die rationale Substanz eingewoben ein sagenhaft emotionaler, herrlich wilder Charakter. Am liebsten würden wir immer noch über die Kurven Kaliforniens räubern und entlang der endlosen Wüstengeraden streunen.

Wie tief die Beziehung zwischen Kalifornien und Porsche ist, zeigt sich übrigens immer wieder bei der Porsche Rennsport Reunion, einem Wochenend-Event auf der legendären Rennstrecke von Laguna Seca: Tausende von Besuchern, Hunderte von klassischen Porsche-Rennwagen im kompromisslosen Infight – selbstverständlich haben wir dort vorbeigeschaut und zeigen Ihnen auf diesen Seiten auch ein paar Eindrücke aus Laguna Seca. Prinzipiell haben wir kaum etwas am CURVES-Charakter geändert: sinnliche Fotos der Straße und der Landschaft sind das Fundament; wir wollen Sie mit auf die Reise nehmen und Ihnen Lust auf diese Reise machen. Die Fotos zeigen dabei unserer Meinung nach nicht nur eine trockene Ansicht, sondern jedes einzelne will auch die Emotion und Atmosphäre der Fahrt vermitteln. Ob wir das geschafft haben, interessiert uns – nehmen Sie doch gerne unter curves-magazin.com Kontakt mit uns auf.

Einen anderen Aspekt der bisherigen CURVES-Ausgaben haben wir nicht fortgesetzt. CURVES Kalifornien wird nicht mehr aus der Ich-Perspektive, als Momentaufnahme erzählt, sondern aus einer zeitlosen Vogel-Perspektive. Ein wenig wie unsere Helikopter-Luftbilder. Wir waren der Meinung, dass das besser zu Kalifornien passt. Am Ende hatten wir eigentlich nur eine Frage: Müsste CURVES denn jetzt nicht besser STRAIGHTS heißen? Aber dann haben wir irgendwo im Death Valley verstanden, dass CURVES ja ein relativer Titel ist. Die Erdoberfläche ist eine Kurve. Welcher Name könnte also besser passen? Viel Freude mit CURVES Kalifornien!

ideas, in questioning set codes, in experimentation. Anybody in Europe who drives thousands of kilometers simply for the pleasure of being on the move is regarded with a degree of suspicion. In the USA, soulful drivers are greeted with understanding and enthusiasm. This is supposedly because the old settler mentality, with its curiosity about the land over the horizon, is still lodged somewhere in the collective consciousness. Freedom is therefore the individual desire to let yourself go with the flow – and in the production of CURVES California, we have dedicated ourselves utterly and without restraint to this desire. Sixty years after a young actor called James Dean tore through the heart of California in his small, purist Porsche in search of the heartbeat of freedom, we did something similar with the new Porsche 911. And as well as unleashing our inner James Dean, we also experienced the fervent love affair that Californians have with Porsche. It's hard to believe how well this ingenious, very German car fits in with the California lifestyle. Woven into the substance is an unbelievably emotional, wonderfully wild character. If we had our way, we would still be storming through the curves of California and roaming along its endless desert straights.

Incidentally, the depth of the relationship between California and Porsche is plain to see again and again at the Porsche Rennsport Reunion, a weekend event at the legendary Laguna Seca race track. Thousands of visitors throng to see hundreds of classic Porsche race cars battling it out. We obviously stopped by, and also have a few images to show you from Laguna Seca.

In principle, we have changed almost nothing of the character of CURVES – sensual photos of road and landscape remain its foundation. We want to take you along on the journey with us and make you feel like doing it too. We think these photos show more than just a dry perspective. Instead, each one of them seeks also to convey the emotion and atmosphere of the drive. We'd like to know whether we've managed to achieve that or not – feel free to get in touch with us on curves-magazin.com. There's another aspect of the previous editions of CURVES that we haven't carried forward into this one. CURVES California is not told from a snapshot perspective as a road trip diary per se, but rather from a timeless bird's eye view – a little like our helicopter images from the air. We reckoned this was a better fit for California.

In the end, we only had one question: Shouldn't CURVES actually now be called STRAIGHTS? But then, somewhere in Death Valley, we understood that CURVES is a relative title. The surface of the earth is curved. So what name could possibly be better suited? We hope you enjoy CURVES California!

KALIFORNIEN • USA

KALIFORNIEN • USA

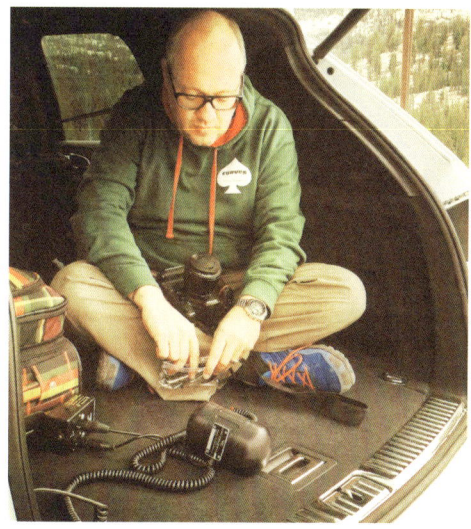

KALIFORNIEN • USA

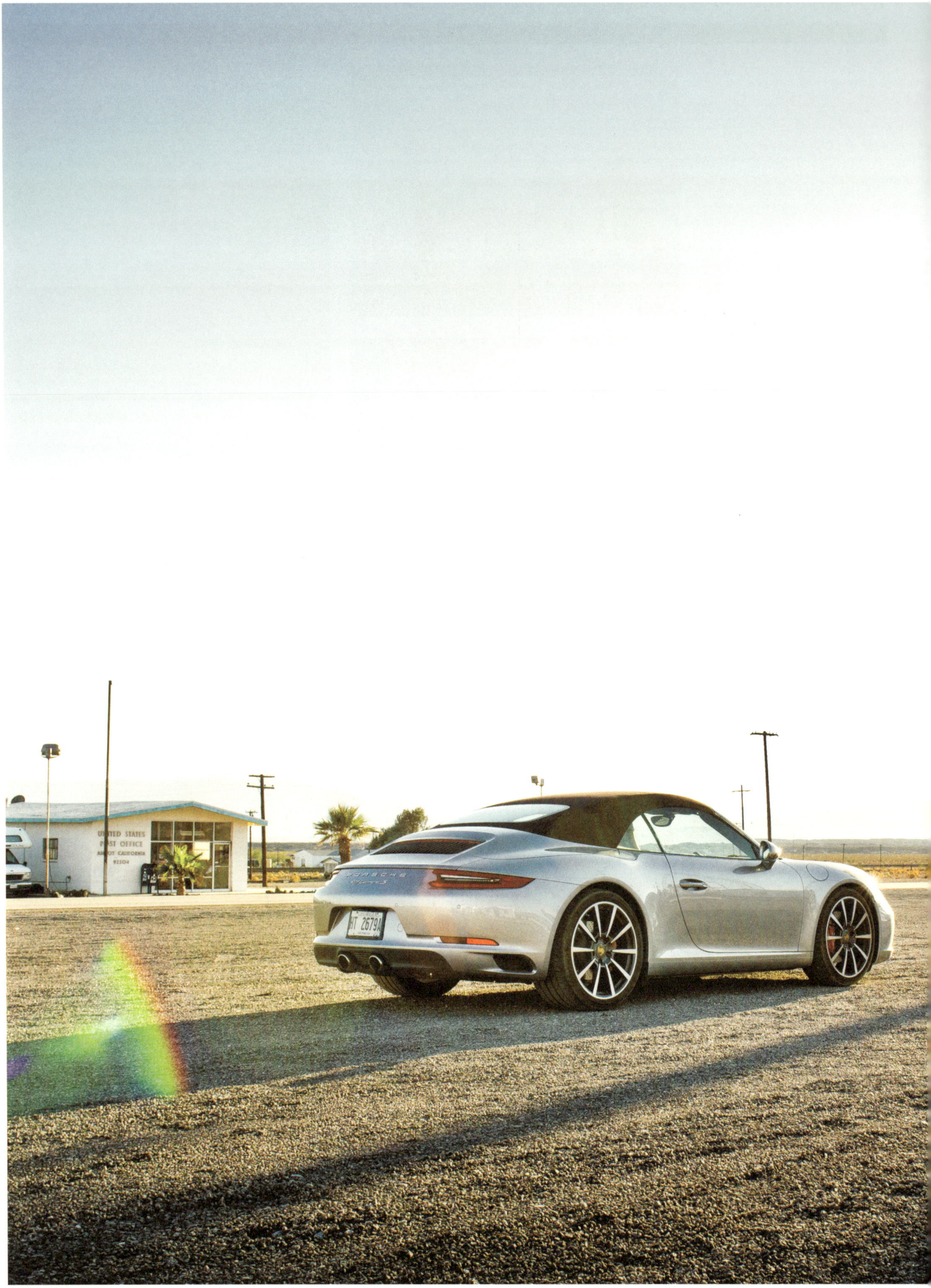
STATES
OFFICE
CALIFORNIA
92304

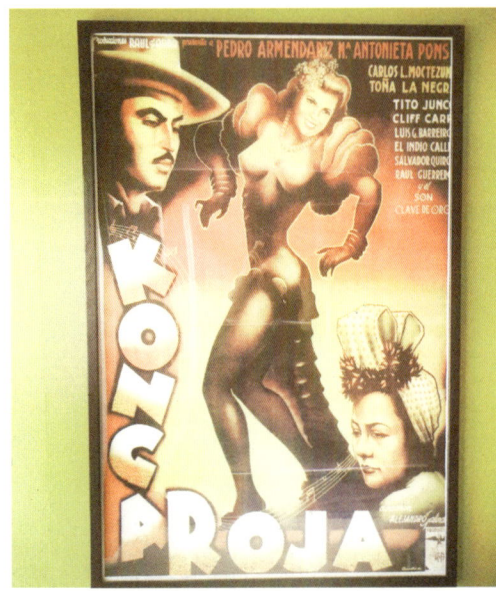

KALIFORNIEN • USA

KALIFORNIEN · USA

DANK AN / THANKS TO
MICHAEL DAIMINGER, BEN WINTER, MARCO BRINKMANN, EDWIN BAASKE, DR. STEPHANIE MAIR-HUYDTS, AXEL SCHILDT, SEBASTIAN WAGNER, MICHAEL DORN, ALEXANDER FAILING, MICHAELA BOGNER, ANDRE OOSTHUIZEN, SCOTT BAKER, MARK FRUECHTNICHT, SCOTT DEVAULT, AMANDA JENSEN, CALVIN KIM, JAMES LONGSTAFFE, ELLYN WUJCIK, ROB RESETAR, STEPHAN SCHUBERT, LUTZ MEDER, NADINE TOBERER

SPECIAL FX / SPECIAL FX
ELENA HERRMANN, ANDREAS HENKE, TIM MAXEINER, LUFTHANSA, DEL RIO AVIATION, HORST PRATSCH, SUNDANCE HELICOPTERS LAS VEGAS & JEAN CLEMENT

COPYRIGHT: Das Werk einschließlich aller seiner Teile ist urheberrechtlich geschützt. Jede Verwertung außerhalb der engen Grenzen des Urheberrechtsgesetzes bedarf der Zustimmung des Urhebers und des Verlags. Die im Inhalt genannten Personen und Handlungen sind frei erfunden. Sollten Ähnlichkeiten mit tatsächlich existenten Personen oder stattgefundenen Handlungen entstanden sein, oder sollte ein solcher Eindruck entstehen, so ist dies unsererseits auf keinen Fall gewollt oder beabsichtigt. Die in diesem Magazin enthaltenen Angaben wurden nach bestem Wissen erstellt. Trotzdem sind inhaltliche und sachliche Fehler nicht vollständig auszuschließen. Deshalb erfolgen alle Angaben ohne Garantie des Verlags und der Autoren. Für die Inhalte übernehmen wir keinerlei Gewähr oder Verantwortung. COPYRIGHT: All rights reserved. No part of this work may be reproduced or used in any form or by any means - without written permission from the author and the publisher. Any mentioned person and/or actions are fictitious. Should there be any similarity to a real existing person or an action, or should such an impression could be originated, it has not been the intention by any means. All information published in this magazine have been produced to the best of one's knowledge. Nevertheless, mistakes regarding contents and objectivity cannot be eliminated completely. Therefore, all the specifications can only be published without guarantee from the publisher's and the author's side. For the contents, there will be no warranty or guarantee.

Porsche 911 Carrera Modelle / Porsche 911 Carrera models:

Kraftstoffverbrauch (in l/100 km)*: innerorts 12,6–9,9 · außerorts 6,9–6,0 · kombiniert 9,0–7,4; CO_2-Emissionen: 208–169 g/km.*
Fuel consumption (in l/100 km)*: urban 12.6–9.9 · extra urban 6.9–6.0 · combined 9.0–7.4; CO_2 emissions: 208–169 g/km.*

*Die angegebenen Werte wurden nach dem vorgeschriebenen Messverfahren (§ 2 Nr. 5, 6, 6a Pkw-EnVKV in der jeweils geltenden Fassung) ermittelt.
*Data determined in accordance with the measurement method specified by Section 2 No. 5, 6, 6a of the German Ordinance on the Energy Consumption Labelling of Passenger Cars (PkW-EnVKV) in the version currently applicable.

IMPRESSUM / IMPRINT

HERAUSGEBER/
PUBLISHER: CURVES MAGAZIN
THIERSCHSTRASSE 25
D-80538 MÜNCHEN

VERANTWORTLICH FÜR
DEN HERAUSGEBER/
RESPONSIBLE FOR
PUBLICATION:
STEFAN BOGNER

KONZEPT/CONCEPT:
STEFAN BOGNER
THIERSCHSTRASSE 25
D-80538 MÜNCHEN
SB@CURVES-MAGAZIN.COM

DELIUS KLASING
CORPORATE PUBLISHING
SIEKERWALL 21
D-33602 BIELEFELD

REDAKTION/
EDITORIAL CONTENT:
EDWIN BAASKE
MARCO BRINKMANN
STEFAN BOGNER
BEN WINTER

ART DIRECTION, LAYOUT, FOTOS/
ART DIRECTION, LAYOUT, PHOTOS:
STEFAN BOGNER
FOTOS MAKING OF/
PHOTOS MAKING-OF:
MICHAEL DAIMINGER

TEXT/TEXT: BEN WINTER
VORWORT/FOREWORD:
ANDREAS HENKE

MOTIVAUSARBEITUNG
LITHOGRAPHIE/SATZ/
POST-PRODUCTION,
LITHOGRAPHY/SETTING:
MICHAEL DORN

KARTENMATERIAL/MAP MATERIAL:
MAIRDUMONT
MARCO-POLO-STR. 1,
73760 OSTFILDERN (KEMNAT)

ÜBERSETZUNG/TRANSLATION
ELAINE CATTON – WHITE PINE
COMMUNICATIONS

PRODUKTIONSLEITUNG/
PRODUCTION MANAGEMENT:
JÖRN HEESE

DRUCK/PRINT:
KUNST- UND WERBEDRUCK
BAD OEYNHAUSEN

2. AUFLAGE
ISBN 978-3-667-11931-5

AUSGEZEICHNET MIT / AWARDED WITH
DDC GOLD - DEUTSCHER DESIGNER CLUB E.V. FÜR GUTE GESTALTUNG // IF COMMUNICATION DESIGN AWARD 2012
BEST OF CORPORATE PUBLISHING // ADC BRONZE // RED DOT BEST OF THE BEST & D&AD // NOMINIERT FÜR
DEN DEUTSCHEN DESIGNPREIS 2015 // WINNER AUTOMOTIVE BRAND CONTEST 2014 // GOOD DESIGN AWARD 2014

CURVES AUSGABEN / OTHER ISSUES OF CURVES

PYRENÄEN / PYRENEES — Im Handel erhältlich/Available in stores
ÖSTERREICH / AUSTRIA — Im Handel erhältlich/Available in stores
SCHWEIZ / SWITZERLAND — Im Handel erhältlich/Available in stores
SCHOTTLAND / SCOTLAND — Im Handel erhältlich/Available in stores
FRANKREICH / FRANCE — Im Handel erhältlich/Available in stores
USA · PART 2 / USA · PART 2 — Im Handel erhältlich/Available in stores
SIZILIEN / SICILY — Im Handel erhältlich/Available in stores
NORDITALIEN / NORTHERN ITALY — Im Handel erhältlich/Available in stores
DEUTSCHLAND/DÄNE. / GERMANY/DENMARK — Im Handel erhältlich/Available in stores
SPANIEN MALLORCA / SPAIN MALLORCA — Im Handel erhältlich/Available in stores